BUT
GOD

BUT
GOD

CHANGES EVERYTHING

HERBERT COOPER

 ZONDERVAN®

ZONDERVAN

But God
Copyright © 2014 by Herbert Cooper

This title is also available as a Zondervan ebook.
Visit www.zondervan.com/ebooks.

Requests for information should be addressed to:
Zondervan, 3900 *Sparks Dr. SE, Grand Rapids, Michigan* 49546

ISBN 978-0-310-33892-5

Herbert Cooper is represented by Thomas J. Winters of Winters & King, Inc.,
Tulsa, Oklahoma.

Interior design: Beth Shagene
Editorial: Sandra Vander Zicht, Jane Haradine, Lauren Niswonger

First printing November 2014 / Printed in the United States of America

To my amazing Lord and Savior Jesus Christ:

Thank you for rescuing me.
Your radical love, grace, and mercy
have brought me a mighty long way.
My life is truly summed up in these two words,
but God.
I'll serve and worship you for all of eternity!

Contents

Foreword

It's amazing how quickly life can take a turn. One moment everything is normal; the next minute everything can change. My family knows this all too well. After my wife, Amy, gave birth to our second child, we were on top of the world. That was until she began to feel weak and frail, and the right side of her body went completely numb. Days turned into weeks. Weeks turned into months. And we still couldn't find any answers for the numbness. Panic set in.

If you live long enough, you'll realize that life can be extremely tough. You might receive a phone call with bad news about someone you love. Or maybe you find out your company is downsizing, and you're likely to lose your job. Maybe your trusted friend betrays you and leaves you wondering how you'll ever heal.

Chances are good that you might be facing one or more challenges right now. You might be enduring the dire consequences of something you did or said that you regret but can't change. You could be trying to climb out of a financial hole that seems too deep to ever overcome. You might be licking your wounds, struggling with bitterness after someone misled you, lied to you, or betrayed you. You could be experiencing health issues that have you paralyzed with fear, wondering what will happen to you.

What do you do when you don't know what to do? So many people try to escape the pain with mindless hours — watching TV, perusing social media in front of a screen, reaching for the dulling effects of alcohol or drugs. Others get mad, vowing never to risk again. Some are tempted to quit on people, on school, on church, or even quit on God. It's easy for the excuses to pile up:

- I know I need to go to the doctor, BUT I don't want to face the news.
- I should forgive him, BUT I am still so angry.
- I really need to change, BUT I've tried and tried and simply can't do it.
- I should trust God, BUT I feel better when I take control.

If you feel like you're up against an obstacle too big to overcome, you are going to absolutely love Pastor Herbert Cooper's life-changing book based on two simple words: But God.

When you stop saying, "But I," and start saying, "But God," everything changes. And that's exactly what my good friend Herbert will teach you to do. Honestly, I don't know anyone better equipped to empower people with this simple, yet game-changing truth.

Without a doubt, Herbert's story is a "But God" story. And that's one of the many reasons I love him. With all he endured early in life, he never should have had a strong marriage — but God made it possible. No one would have thought that he'd become a role model for everyone from professional athletes to grade school students, but God made a way. On his own, he would have found it almost impossible to forgive those who hurt him — but what is impossible with people is possible with God. Herbert unquestionably never would have guessed he would become a pastor — but God changed him and opened doors no person could open. And now he's one of the most effective men of God I know.

If you're wondering what happened to my wife and her health concerns, I'm thankful to tell you we had a "But God" moment. After seeing doctor after doctor and taking more tests than we could count, we still didn't have answers, and Amy's health continued to decline. One day as Amy was doing her daily devotional, she had a spiritual epiphany and put her whole trust in God. If God healed her, she would trust him. If he didn't, she would trust him. No matter what, she committed her life, her family, and her future wholly to her Savior.

Nothing on the outside changed, but God did something only he could do. Her heart was at peace, and as quickly as her problems had appeared, they were gone. She had been declining physically, but God made her well. I am so thankful that no matter what we face, God can make a way.

You may have any number of legitimate reasons why you won't make it through what you are facing or achieve what you've dreamed, but two words can change every-thing. No matter how hopeless your situation looks or how discouraged you are, remember ...

But God changes everything.

CRAIG GROESCHEL

Two Little Words

My flesh and my heart may fail, but God is the
strength of my heart and my portion forever.

PSALM 73:26

Just two little words.

Two little words changed the course of history. They are short, simple, one-syllable words that we don't often think about putting together. And yet, when they are paired, they remind us of a truth bigger than any trial, any trouble, or any turmoil in which we find ourselves. These two words have changed countless lives throughout history; they changed my life, and they can change yours. If you've noticed the title of this book, then you already know them.

But God ...

They are deceptively simple. In grammatical terms, *but* functions as a conjunction, joining one thought (or independent clause for you grammar junkies) with another. Each time *but* appears, a contrast, qualification, or counter-argument follows. In other words, the second part of the sentence is going to be different from the first.

Okay, thanks for the seventh-grade language arts review, you may be thinking, *but so what?* But *"what?"* is indeed the question. And another little three-letter word answers it like no other: but *God*!

God supplies the contrast to our limitations, liabilities, and losses. He turns our expectations upside down, blows our minds, and transforms our hearts with the ways he loves us, protects us, provides for us, and redeems us.

This little phrase "but God" occurs multiple times in the Bible — more than three dozen, depending on your translation (see Appendix). Each time, these two little words reveal that a divine change is about to occur in human lives. Just consider ...

A married couple long to have a child but know they're too old to conceive ...

A frightened crowd begs a naive teenager not to fight a bully three times his size ...

A messenger fears for his life after abandoning the route he should have taken ...

A few dozen men face an army of thousands ...

A pair of widows return to one's homeland, wracked with grief and certain of their impoverished future ...

A boy is sold into slavery, then is imprisoned on false charges ...

A young, innocent woman cannot imagine being with child since she has never known a man ...

A body is placed in a tomb and sealed with a stone ...

In each case, it's the difference between a human perspective and God's viewpoint. What looks impossible to us becomes not only possible but easy for God. When you have a "but God" moment in your life, what follows that moment will be drastically different from what came before it.

There's no easy way to define "but God" changes, but you always know when you encounter them. Sometimes God intervenes and everything literally changes in a single moment, like Saul becoming blind on the road to Damascus and becoming Paul, or Jesus healing the sick with a touch of his hand. Other "but God" transformations occur over time—days, weeks, months, even years—and require ongoing faith as God fulfills his promise. Abraham and Sarah waiting to conceive. Hannah desperately begging for a son. Joseph enduring a lifetime of injustice before rising to power as Pharaoh's right-hand man and reuniting with his family.

Sometimes God meets us in dramatic revelations, and we experience a "but God" moment instantly. Other times we simply experience the quiet assurance of his presence, protection, and provision during difficulties and challenging seasons of life. Often we don't even see God's intervention until we look back. In hindsight, we see how God showed up, sustained us, helped us, healed us, directed us, led us, and provided for us. The change didn't occur overnight, but God definitely showed up and transformed our situation—and drew us closer to him in the process. No matter if it happens instantly or takes years to recognize, a "but God" experience changes everything.

These meetings often emerge out of our life circumstances and our willingness to look for God's direction in the midst of losing our way. In many situations, we come to a point when we seem to hit a dead end. It may be sudden and unexpected, like turning a corner and running into a brick wall. Or it may be a treadmill of same-old, same-old, running back and forth, here and there, work-home-school-church, but getting nowhere. Maybe it's wandering through the labyrinth of life each day, looking for a way out of the disappointing maze of the mundane.

If you've ever lost a job or listened in shock as a doctor shared test results, then you know what I'm talking about. If you've ever become hooked on something that slowly tried to destroy you, then you know the fear, the shame, the powerlessness I'm talking about. If you've ever come home to find evidence of your spouse's betrayal, then you know about pain and loneliness, confusion and anger. Maybe there's no big secret in your closet or crisis looming on the horizon, but you still feel tired, weary, longing for something more than what you have.

Sooner or later, we all come to a point where our lives have to change. We can rarely see beyond our immediate circumstances to envision a solution. We can't imagine anything positive ever coming from what we're facing. But no matter how bleak, boring, or bitter your life may seem right now, your story is not over yet.

You think one thing, but God knows another.

You feel trapped, but God can free you.

You see no way out, but God provides a way.

You hunger for more, but God satisfies you beyond your wildest dreams.

You fear change, but God alone is the same yesterday, today, and forever.

Whatever your first-half phrase might be, "but God" opens up new possibilities, ones you can't even imagine. The phrase is short, but the implications are huge. Throughout this book, I would like to convince you that change is possible by sharing my own "but God" experiences, similar encounters I've witnessed in the lives of my family, and some of the powerful "but God" interventions we see in Scripture.

I also want to help you see beyond the barriers that get in our way. To experience a more authentic faith that's vital, active, and risky. To drop the old baggage you've been carrying around and pick up your purpose. To dream bigger and dare to hope again. To reach out to others and surprise them with the love, grace, and power of a God who challenges the conventional, the traditional, the rational, and the logical.

Two little words.

The divine pivot point that changes everything.

You only think you know what he's up to.

But God . . .

1

We Wander ...
But God Finds Us

But God demonstrates his own love for us in this:
While we were still sinners, Christ died for us.

ROMANS 5:8

Wewoka, Oklahoma, is the kind of town where teenage
excitement on the weekend consists of cruising the main
drag in your pickup truck (cool), your parents' SUV (not
so cool), or a friend's pimped-up hatchback (the coolest).
I'm proud to say that growing up there, I knew every
dusty square inch of asphalt from the IGA supermarket
at one end all the way to the mini-mart convenience store
and gas station a couple miles down the road. Of course,
this was back when gas was 89 cents a gallon, and you
could afford to drive around without a reason.

High school football and basketball games captured everyone's attention, along with the team's record and stats on its star players. Otherwise, there wasn't much going on. Needless to say, when teens go looking for fun in a small town, they sometimes find it in the wrong places or create their own out of the perceived building blocks of bliss: alcohol, drugs, partying, and sex. For some reason, I never cared about alcohol or drugs, but I had my own form of searching for fun. As one of the star athletes of the football team, my full-time job was working on my image as a player off the field as much as I was one on the field. I chased girls, pumped my mind full of filthy music, dabbled in pornography, and engaged in sex outside of marriage with numerous young women.

Although it seemed exciting at first, it became exhausting to maintain this lifestyle. I had to always think about how I looked and how others might view me. It was like leading a double life. Yet I couldn't let go of the importance of making sure my peers viewed me a certain way — you know, cool beyond cool, original but standing out only for the right reasons, a man all the guys envied and all the women wanted to be with.

As a result, I made sure everything I did added to this persona — like rolling up to the school parking lot in the mornings, windows down, bass pumpin', hip-hop blastin', making sure everyone knew I was *there*. Yes, I was well liked, but honestly, I knew it and it showed. I was not only a bit too sexy for my shirt (remember that song?), but for my jeans and leather Nikes as well!

Part of my need to build up my image stemmed from how vulnerable I felt on the inside. I wanted to make sure stories about my upbringing and home life never made it to the school grapevine. The events sound like last week's episode of *The Real Housewives of Wewoka*. I'll try to fill you in on my world then.

Turning Points

My mom and dad's marriage was the second for both of them. My older half brother, who lived with us, resulted from my mom's previous marriage. My father had two kids from previous relationships, but they were fifteen or twenty years older than I was and lived in a different city, so we didn't see them much. And then I had a sister who was eleven months younger than I was.

So growing up, we three kids shared the house, and we were close. I shared a room and bunk beds with my older brother until he moved out after high school. Every Friday night my mom, sister, brother, and I would have a family burrito night — forget bean burritos, I'm talking BBQ burritos! As much fun as those meals were, though, we eventually had to leave the restaurant and return home. And our home was in shambles.

There, alcoholism and abuse presided. Frequently, my parents exploded into fits of screaming, yelling, and fighting. Aware that an emotional bomb might go off any minute, I constantly dodged land mines of tension, fear, and anger. I even installed a lock on my bedroom door to feel safer while I was at home, but many times, it was just easier for me to leave, to be anywhere else but in the midst of my parents' collateral damage.

So can you see why I felt like two different people?

When I was at home, I felt vulnerable, unsure, afraid. When I was on the football field, at school, or cruising the boulevard, I could create that "cool jock" image. This image gave me a sense of confidence and acceptance, so I worked to maintain it no matter what it took.

During my junior year, my parents went through a horrible split. The time had finally come when my mom decided she needed to leave.

I'll never forget the day I helped her load up her car after my dad left the house. She had decided to take my brother and sister to Rochester, New York, where her sister lived and where she could put thousands of miles between herself and my father.

She wanted me to go with them, of course. And, honestly, being something of a "mama's boy," I was torn.

But I knew that if I wanted any shot at a football scholarship, I had to stay put. I couldn't risk trading the rest of my junior year and senior season at Wewoka for starting over in a place where my talent was unknown.

As I stood watching the car roll away from the house that day, I wondered what life would be like after the people I cared about most were no longer in it. I had chosen to stay with my dad, gambling on a future that remained uncertain, but at least offered the possibility of permanent escape. If I could get noticed by college scouts and offered a football scholarship, then I could leave behind the scared boy I was on the inside and become the cool jock I wanted to be.

That day will forever stand out in my mind. Not just because my mother and siblings moved out, but also because she had left it to me to inform my dad of their departure. When my dad returned home that day and discovered his wife had left him, I saw him cry for one of the few times in my life.

Friday Night Lights

My parents' divorce shattered my world. When I recall the emotions of this part of my past, tears still come to my eyes. This mama's boy had to learn how to cook, clean, do my own laundry, get myself up for school on time, meet my homework deadlines, and do other chores my mom had always done. It was time to grow up — fast — to survive. I felt angry, confused, isolated, and so lonely.

Not only was I trapped by the pursuit of my image, but now my family was torn apart and my heart ached more than ever. I didn't want our home life to continue on as it had been, but neither did I want my mom, brother, and sister living all the way across the country. They had moved in the fall, and I remember waking up on that first Christmas morning without them. If I could have skipped that day, I would have. What was the point of Christmas if our whole family wasn't going to be together? Once one of my favorite times of the year when I'd count down the days until the twenty-fifth, now Christmas was just another day — no, worse, since I felt more miserable than ever.

So I devoted myself to sports — especially football. I couldn't wait to put those pads on. I lived to get out on the field and score a touchdown or grab an interception. It was my outlet, my escape from the pain I was feeling at home. I lived for Thursdays and Fridays when I could wear my jersey to school. I lived for those pep rallies. I lived for Friday nights under the white lights of a cool autumn night. I felt like a winner out there, in control of my destiny, in a world where I belonged.

For a few hours on Friday night, all felt right with the world. Seemed like the whole town showed up to cheer for our team, my dad included. He would scream at the top of his lungs and run back and forth in front of the bleachers, providing some of the affirmation every boy craves from his dad. This game — and all it included — was what I had stayed behind for. But no matter how many touchdowns I scored or how many games our team won, off the field nothing changed. My life was still a mess.

Angry and confused, I continued my lifestyle, not caring much *about* other people — just about what they thought of me. From all outward appearances, I was on a roll: a good student, a star athlete, student council president, National Honor Society member, and never without a beautiful young woman by my side. Most people thought I had it all together — which, as you can imagine, could not be further from the truth. I was actually hanging on by a thread.

One day I found myself in a shouting match with one of my coaches and realized how low I had sunk. Though I can't remember what triggered it, I do remember that I had a bad attitude at practice, and he rightly called me on it. My thinking clouded by my pain, I couldn't understand why the coach would single me out like that. I just kept insisting, "You don't understand what I've been going through! You don't understand!"

Normally, I never would have had an outburst like that, but my volatile emotions just erupted. No one seemed able to look beyond my external facade and figure out what was really going on with me. Football was the only great thing left in my life, and suddenly I was losing control of that too! To top it off, my teammates witnessed my outburst, which went against the carefully crafted cool image I had worked so hard to construct.

I couldn't take much more.

Wandering Alone

I don't know what your story is or how you grew up, but I'm guessing you know what it means to wander without going anywhere. Doesn't matter if you're a star on the high school football field or an executive in a corner office, an unwed mother in a small town or a career mom in the 'burbs, we all create an image of how we want others to see us. We all struggle to know who we really are and why we're here. As we travel down this journey toward discovering who God made us to be, we often take a few detours in pursuit of what we think will fulfill us. When we don't know who we are in Christ, we're prone to experiment, to wander, to get lost along the way.

We rarely want to admit these struggles. We're unhappy, searching for something more, so we wander, trying to find happiness in the wrong things. We look for comfort wherever we can find it, whether in the arms of an illicit lover, or the taste of triple-fudge ice cream, or the thrill of our latest online purchase. Our distractions keep us from asking the hard questions and having an honest conversation with God.

But there's one thing you need to know about the way

God rolls. He will never force you to have a "but God" encounter. He's always present in your life, willing to help you, to welcome you home, to provide for your needs, to comfort and protect you.

But we have to admit that we need him. We have to acknowledge our fear, unhappiness, and loneliness and recognize that we're lost. We have to invite God to butt into our business if we want to experience the healing he wants to bring. This requires telling ourselves, and others around us, the truth. Our most important "but God" experience occurs when we recognize just how empty our lives are without him.

Divine Appointment

I recognized this truth in a high school locker room. At the beginning of my senior year, a scout from an East Coast school scheduled a visit to watch me play. His interest was exactly what I'd been hoping for — the chance to be recruited to play college football. Stopping first in Oklahoma City, he called on the night we were supposed to meet and informed me that he wouldn't arrive in Wewoka until the following day.

My night and plans were blown. I was disappointed, but I tried to be patient and hold myself together. So with nothing else to do that evening, I decided to make an appearance in our locker room for a Fellowship of Christian Athletes meeting. Truth be told, I went because they were serving free pizza. Yep, if you want old Coop to show up, all you have to do is offer a deluxe with extra cheese!

Todd Thompson, former kicker for the Oklahoma

Sooners, was the guest speaker that night. As an avid Sooners fan, I knew who Thompson was, but since I was still angry, hurting, and confused — as well as self-conscious of my precious image — I remained aloof. But despite the protective wall around my battered heart, Thompson commanded my attention.

For one thing, I was surprised to see him simply sit in a chair and speak to us conversationally, rather than jumping up and screaming at us about Jesus or hell or both as I expected. He communicated the simple gospel message: Jesus came, died, and rose again. He explained that all of us have done things that are wrong; no one is innocent or even close to perfect. But God loves us so much that he gave up what was most precious to him — his only Son — as payment for our sins. He cares for us so much that no matter what we've done, he still welcomes us as his sons and daughters.

Listening to Todd talk, I wondered if maybe what I needed was what he was talking about. Here was someone explaining to me that God had made me for something more than what I was chasing. I caught a glimpse of something that felt like that first gulp of air after being underwater for a long time. Hope. Suddenly, I could breathe again for the first time since I was a little kid.

Then I felt tears coursing down my face. I could feel them not just on my cheeks, but landing on my hands, dropping to the floor. Before I knew it, I had passed the point of no return. I wasn't just crying — this was blubbering! And strangest of all, I didn't even care that a locker room full of teammates could see the captain of their football team weeping.

This was *bigger*.

Finally, I found something I wanted more than being cool.

That night, I gave my life to Christ, beginning a complete change in my life. There's no doubt about it. Without that moment, I would have headed down a very different road. Sure, I may have ended up with a football scholarship, yet I would have continued to live a reckless lifestyle that would have destroyed me in the end. But God had a better plan for my college years. I ended up with a football scholarship that helped pay for my education, but I also took an opportunity to transfer to another university to pursue a biblical studies degree. And there I met the woman who became my wife!

Without that life-changing encounter with God in high school, I would not be the man I am now, the man God created me to be. I would not have the amazing family I have now. And I definitely would not have the privilege of pastoring a church — something that not only challenged me but also fulfilled me.

But God had a plan for finding me, a plan that involved a college scout canceling our meeting and a young man's hunger for more than just free pizza. I was lost, wandering from one bad choice to another, but God cared enough about me to schedule a divine appointment in that locker room, an encounter that forever changed my life.

But God Runs to Meet You

I'm certainly not the only one who has had a "but God" moment. As I mentioned earlier, the Bible is full of them.

One of my favorites serves as a good starting point because it reminds us that no matter how far away we may wander, God always runs to meet us. We can be off somewhere doing our own thing, maybe rebelling outright like a prodigal son or daughter, or maybe just trying to make life work on our own terms. But regardless of where we are or what other people think of us, God knows our heart. He knows the desperate loneliness and aching need we carry around inside. He knows our fears and dreams as well as our worst mistakes and best efforts.

One of Jesus' best-known parables captures our Father's love, compassion, and mercy in a simple story of rebellion and reconciliation. An ambitious son, eager to grab life by the tail and enjoy all of the world's pleasures, insults his father and goes off in pursuit of what he thinks will make him happy. But after the money dries up and the parties end, after the friends-for-hire and the groupies fade away, the lost son hits rock bottom. He's lost everything — including his own dignity. Then one day he remembers something that's more powerful than his mistakes:

> "When he came to his senses, he said, 'How many of my father's hired servants have food to spare, and here I am starving to death! I will set out and go back to my father and say to him: Father, I have sinned against heaven and against you. I am no longer worthy to be called your son; make me like one of your hired servants.' So he got up and went to his father.
>
> "*But* while he was still a long way off, his father saw him and was filled with compassion for him; he ran to his son, threw his arms around him and kissed him.

"The son said to him, 'Father, I have sinned
against heaven and against you. I am no longer worthy to be called your son.'

"But the father said to his servants, 'Quick! Bring
the best robe and put it on him. Put a ring on his
finger and sandals on his feet. Bring the fattened calf
and kill it. Let's have a feast and celebrate. For this
son of mine was dead and is alive again; he was lost
and is found.' So they began to celebrate."

LUKE 15:17 – 24, emphasis mine

See the "but God" moments? This busted, disgusted,
frustrated, and brokenhearted young man had to recognize his need in order to come to his senses. He was
tired of chasing his addictions and wandering farther and
farther away from home. He had fallen about as low as
he could imagine falling — from partying like a player to
slopping pigs like a beggar. He must have felt miserable
when he realized his wandering had led to this dead end.
He may even have wondered if he had wandered too far,
if it was too late for his life to change.

Can you relate to this young man's experience? Have
you wandered farther and farther away from where you
want to be? From where God wants you to be? Sometimes
we think that it's too late for us, that we can't change our
life's direction and return to God. We fear we've crossed
a point of no return, that we can never change. But this
is not true. Not only can we change direction, but we can
go home.

At his lowest point, this young man remembers something that pierces through the fog of his depression, frus-

tration, and self-contempt. He remembers his father's character. While the young man believes he's no longer worthy to be called a son, he knows that his father will at least allow him to work in a more respectful environment. He can beg for forgiveness and try to regain his dignity.

So he returns home — tired, hungry, filthy, humbled, and alone. But instead of an angry, judgmental father claiming, "I told you so," the young man sees his dad running to meet him, to hold him, to love him just the way he is. His father is thrilled because his son has come home.

The young man cannot believe how much his father loves him. He knows that his father has every right to be angry, hurt, and justified in holding a grudge. But his father doesn't.

But God doesn't hold grudges against us either. Just the opposite! We're still a long way from home, but God runs out to meet us. We're aware of how we've sinned against him, but God welcomes us with open arms.

You don't have to wander anymore, my friend. No matter what you've done or not done. How high you've risen or how low you've crashed. If you're weary of wandering, then come home. You can keep chasing things you hope will fulfill you, but only God can satisfy the hunger in your heart.

You've wandered far enough.

But God is ready to welcome you home.

Coming Home

I realize you may be thinking, *That's a great story, Herbert — both your own and the prodigal's. But you don't understand what I'm dealing with. I'm not a kid anymore — it's too late for me to change. I've wandered a long, long way from home. Made a lot of mistakes with consequences I'm still paying for. You don't know what I've done or who I am.*

No, I get it. We've all messed up and had our moments of deep personal shame. Maybe it's not sex outside of marriage, but a bitter, hate-filled desire to get back at someone who hurt you. Maybe you abuse alcohol. Maybe you're caught up in cheating and lying. Maybe you find yourself stuck in a web of these sins and even more.

Or maybe your sins are subtler and seemingly not as severe. You smile in front of your friend at church but gossip about her at work. You look at images online that ignite your lust. You secretly wish harm to your abusive boss. In case you don't realize it, you're still wandering. You need a "but God" moment just as much as anyone else.

Maybe you feel like your life is falling apart. You're portraying one thing on the outside and living something else on the inside. Maybe you present yourself as one person in public, but in private you are completely different. Maybe you are going through the motions of a life that's not what you hoped it would be. You're chasing money, success, relationships, sex, status symbols — anything to help you escape the truth of what you need the most.

You need something to happen in your life.

You need a "but God" moment.

You need to come home.

Ever since that night in a high school locker room when I decided to give the rest of my life to God, he has taken every area of my life and turned it around, blessing it in ways I could never have imagined – personal relationships, parenting, career choices, to name only a few. These two little words have radically changed the direction of my life. I'm no longer wandering around, trying to pretend that I've got it together, secretly wondering who I am and why I'm here.

If you need a new direction in your life, if you need a change, if you need a radical breakthrough, if you need to break free from an addiction, if you need the old to go and the new to come, if you're tired of wandering away from the very purpose for which you were created, then you've picked up the right book. While your most important "but God" encounter comes down to the moment when you choose to let him into your life, the process of transformation usually occurs over time. Your salvation is secured instantly, but the process of becoming more like Jesus is lived out day to day.

You feel lost and alone ... but God knows and cares for you. These two words can make your "after" radically different from your "before."

You feel lost and broken, but God sees you and knows your heart. He loves you and wants to change you. He's calling you in from where you've been wandering. He's calling you to stand before him and accept your divine destiny, to become the person he created you to be for the purpose that you alone can fulfill. He loves you and wants to welcome you home, to heal your heart, and to transform you into the person you were meant to be.

Will you let him?

2

We're Wounded ...
But God Heals Us

He heals the brokenhearted
and binds up their wounds.

PSALM 147:3

The first time it happened, I was thirteen years old. I remember thinking, *What was that? It has to be wrong! But it felt good ... does that make me a horrible person? Should I tell my parents what happened? Will they believe me?* An uncomfortable mix of fear, shame, and confusion enveloped me. *Why did this happen? And what should I do about it?*

It doesn't take long to learn that hurt comes in all kinds of forms. It hurts when you make a mistake and cause pain for someone you care about. It hurts when you get into an argument with someone. It hurts to get passed over for a job promotion. It hurts if you find out someone you trusted has been talking behind your back.

But some wounds run deeper than others. Sometimes we experience the greatest amount of pain when something happens that never should have occurred in the first place — something we had no control over.

Silent Misery

This is the kind of wound I experienced at thirteen when an adult female sexually molested me. As a friend of our family, she came over regularly, which meant this abuse was not a one-time event. My parents had no idea and obviously trusted this woman, which only compounded my fear and shame. Somehow it felt like my fault, but how could that be true?

The molestation occurred over several months. Whenever I'd walk into a room where this woman was present, I'd churn inside with a sick sense of dread and negative anticipation. As a teen too young to get his license, it wasn't like I could just drive off and leave whenever I encountered her. Before long, I wondered and worried every day when I would have to face her again.

Finally, after months of dealing with this misery, I worked up the courage to tell this woman to leave me alone. To say I was terrified is an understatement; after all, she was the grown-up, someone I had once liked and respected. With a shaky voice, I told her, "I don't want this to continue. Please leave me alone."

We stood next to one another in a doorway, with our

backs turned so that no one would overhear us. At first she tilted her head and spoke softly, "I want to be with you. I care about you." My body began to shake, maybe from fear, maybe from anxiety. Through tears, once again I said, "Please leave me alone."

This time the tenderness in her voice turned to rage. "This relationship *is* going to continue because if you cut this off, I'll tell your parents about us. About how you started this."

Stunned, I felt my knees almost buckle beneath me.

Looking back now as an adult, I know that, of course, she wasn't going to tell anyone and expose her crime. But at the time, I was terrified and felt so very alone. Nonetheless, I stood my ground.

With renewed determination, I firmly said, "Then tell them. But this is over." I shut the door in her face, collapsed on my bed, and began to sob. I had such fear in my heart that my parents would find out. And I felt so confused, which only made the ache inside more intense. But the abuse stopped. She left me alone.

Those months have forever affected my life. I developed a poor view of women. I fostered a great mistrust for people. The abuse resulted in my harboring anger and hostility, insecurity, and shame. Becoming sexually active at such a young age also propelled me down a road of promiscuity. Like an old war injury that continues to ache long after the battle has ended, my wound reverberated across many years of my life.

I would have remained broken and ashamed, but God healed my wound and restored my heart. The healing has been a process, not an instant overnight change like

I sometimes hoped. Nevertheless, his faithfulness, grace, and love have filled that hurt inside me where something had been taken away at such a young age.

The Process of Healing

Without a doubt, some of you reading this have suffered your own kind of hurt and damage. Like me, you may have been sexually abused as a child. Sadly, one in four girls and one in six boys will be abused before the age of eighteen.

Or perhaps you were emotionally abused by listening to a barrage of negative ideas about yourself from your parents while growing up. Maybe someone close to you betrayed you. Maybe your parents divorced, or perhaps a friend or family member lied to you about an important issue. Maybe your spouse has been unfaithful, or maybe you have suffered physical or sexual abuse from someone who was supposed to love and care for you. In whatever package your hurt arrived, the consequences can include anything from trust issues to a fear of intimacy to bitterness to limitless other challenges. If you've dealt with a major hurt in your life, it's likely controlled your life since it happened. If you don't take the steps to deal with it, it could keep controlling your future as well.

But God tells us that we don't have to remain wounded and suffering, limping along in pain and misery. You can be free of your hurt. You can recover emotionally. You can prevent this hurt from controlling your decisions and directions. You may still bear the scars, but God can heal you.

After my experience, I carried around unhealthy

thoughts and emotions for years. But eventually I realized that in order to have a better future, I was going to have to work through the hurt from my past. And I couldn't deal with it all by myself. My "but God" encounter in this area has been slow and steady. After I gave my heart to God and accepted Jesus as my Savior, I began the process of restoration. While each person's recovery may be unique, taking certain steps often allows God's healing presence to begin the process. Let me share with you the ones that were instrumental in my "but God" healing.

Removing Fig Leaves

Based on my own experience, I suspect we frequently try to hide our wounds from God. Whether our wound is from something that was done to us or from something sinful that we've selfishly pursued, we avoid coming before God. We begin to believe the lies of our enemy and wonder if God can love us after what we've experienced. After all, if we can't love ourselves, how could God, who's perfect and holy, love us?

Apparently, it's our human nature, dating back to the first time it happened with our first parents. After they blew it, Adam and Eve tried to hide their shame and guilt from God too. When they ate the forbidden fruit that God specifically instructed them to leave alone, they tried to hide in the garden. Not only did they hide, but they also covered their nakedness — something once beautifully innocent that now brought them shame — with fig leaves. They tried to hide who they were and what they had done from their Creator.

It seems absurd when we read that story now. Really? God's not going to see them hiding behind those bushes? He's not going to notice the new his-and-her green outfits? How did they think they could possibly hide from God? Yet as crazy as it may seem for Adam and Eve to hide from the all-knowing, all-seeing God, we do the same from time to time.

We put our own fig leaves over our wounds and try to cover up our transgressions. Instead of running to the one who can forgive and heal us, we push God away. We don't want to let him into our personal pain and major messes. Yet Jesus came to earth to be in the middle of your mess: "The LORD is close to the brokenhearted and saves those who are crushed in spirit" (Ps. 34:18).

If you feel God wouldn't want any part of your brokenness, or you feel that because of what happened to you in your past you are not worthy of asking him into your trouble, you need to think again. God wants to be there! He wants to help you! The Bible tells us, "By his wounds we are healed" (Isa. 53:5). *His* wounds — not ours! Without the Lord's healing power, our pain can cause us to lash out. You see, wounded people wound others, whether they intend to or not.

Don't stiff-arm God. Give up that pain. Your wounds and your past do not shock him. He knows, he understands, and he will help you. If you want to experience the healing of a "but God" encounter, then invite him into your secrets, your issues, and your pain, and see what happens.

I'm a living example that God draws near to the brokenhearted. He's healed my life and my heart. Today I am whole. Not perfect by any means, but *whole*. I get to love God, love people, love my wife, my kids, and my church. As I've stressed, God did not heal me overnight. "But God" encounters can happen in the blink of an eye, or they can take place over time, especially when they involve allowing God to heal our deepest wounds.

The Healing Presence of God

Another key factor in my healing was cultivating a deeper relationship with God. In fact, the way I've experienced his healing presence the most is by spending time with him — *in his Word, in prayer, and in worship.* Before I became a Christian and began practicing my faith, I was bitter and mad at the world — yelling at my coach, being a jerk to my friends, acting disrespectful to my parents, and acting out sexually. I was much more concerned about appearances than what was going on inside my heart. Although my life looked radically different after that locker room encounter with God, I discovered that the more time I spent learning about, talking to, and praising God, the more peace, joy, and healing I experienced in my heart.

At first, I learned to set aside time each day to spend reading the Bible, meditating on its meaning, application, and truth in my life. I realized that prayer is as simple as talking directly to God, having a conversation with him throughout each day. And worship is the combination of our gratitude, appreciation, and recognition of who God is and what he's done for us. It too became a part of my "daily diet." Each practice is vitally important, but together they provide a soothing balm filled with the peace that passes understanding. Let's consider each one in a little more detail.

I cannot overstate the importance of the *Word*. Like bread for the starving and water for the parched, the Bible provides powerful healing to us as we encounter God's timeless truth. We're told, "He sent out his word and healed them; he rescued them from the grave" (Ps. 107:20). The Word has healing power! The Bible is not just an ordinary book. It's not just historical literature with lots of stories and poems. It's called the "living Word" because it is alive, it penetrates the heart, and it heals!

If you're going through pain or trauma, then fall in love with the Word. Consume it daily. As a young adult trying to experience healing, I was so hungry for the Word of God that I read through the Bible four or five times. I devoured it even as it changed and delivered me.

So many verses reveal how God is a healer and lifts us up when we are weak. One verse in particular never ceased to refresh and strengthen me: "[God] heals the brokenhearted and binds up their wounds" (Ps. 147:3). I was hurt and broken, and reading that verse helped lessen the pain I felt.

Prayer is also so important to the healing process. We are told many times in the Bible that God hears us: "If ... they cry out to me, I will certainly hear their cry" (Ex. 22:23). God hears our anguish and our pain. When we're distraught, he's there to heal our broken hearts. Some of the most well-known prayers in the Bible are from David, a powerful leader who wrote heartfelt prayers and songs. He reminds us that we can pray anytime: "Evening, morning and noon I cry out in distress, and he hears my voice"

(Ps. 55:17). David also demonstrated that we can express every emotion in prayer — our anger, our fear, our confusion, and our despair — not just our joy and gratitude.

Like David, I cried out to God with all of my pain, hurt, abuse, and confusion. Instead of turning to sex, as I had in the past, I turned to the Lord. I called to the Lord, and he continued to heal my heart. I was broken, but prayer opened my heart to God and his healing power.

And finally, *worship* played a huge part in my healing. I can remember my freshman year in college at Arkansas Tech. I was there on a football scholarship, and a lot of my teammates were partiers, chasing the girls. Instead of joining them, I'd drive around in my car on Friday nights, headed for the Burger King, having a private worship session there in my car.

When I transferred to Oral Roberts University my sophomore year, I'd sit in my dorm room, listening to Kirk Franklin's album *God Is Able.* I would sing along: "I sing because I'm happy, I sing because I'm free. His eye is on the sparrow, and I know he watches me." These early, intimate worship times I had with God drew me closer to him and, again, opened my heart to his healing. I can't overstate it: I would not be who I am today if I hadn't had these moments with God through reading his Word, in prayer, and in worship. These are key ingredients in receiving his healing power. So is forgiveness.

Forgive to Move Forward

Healing from deep wounds involves forgiving those who have hurt and betrayed you. Easier said than done, right?

When someone wrongs us, we feel justified in our anger and bitterness. Some of us walk around for years spewing hate about the person in our past.

Yes, forgiveness is hard, but hate is harder. I'm not telling you this as a biblically based pastor; I'm telling you from my own experience. Holding on to a grudge is harder than letting it go. It takes a lot more energy to carry around that anger than to release it. Ironically, the person who caused the pain often ends up walking around with no repercussions!

No matter how justified we feel in our judgment, hatred, and condemnation of the person who wounded us, in the end we're all sinners needing repair. By and through the grace of God, not one of us gets what we deserve. We're all damaged, looking for redemption. But it doesn't end there.

Once we have been saved, it's not okay to keep sinning because of the grudges we carry. We're called — no, commanded — to love and forgive others the same way God loves and forgives us. We're told, "Forgive as the Lord forgave you" (Col. 3:13). As hard as it was to forgive my abuser, I pray she is able to experience grace at the foot of the cross not only for her redemption, but also so she can forgive someone who likely abused her in the same way.

When we decide not to forgive, it is like going through life carrying around a dumbbell. But instead of making you stronger, it just makes you weary. Holding on to anger cannot do anything beneficial for you, but letting go of anger can. So many times people hold a grudge, and when they finally decide to forgive, they realize they had imprisoned themselves, not the other person, with their anger. Forgiveness unlocks the door to your own freedom. There is something cathartic in letting go of the bitterness and anger that you've been holding on to for so long.

Boundaries of Forgiveness

After I committed my life to Christ, I knew I was forgiven, yet it was still hard to forgive the woman who had abused me. For a while it was easier just to try to not think about it. But eventually, I knew that to experience a "but God" encounter, to experience all that God had for me, I had to forgive.

The Bible says that if we have truly experienced God's forgiveness, then we will be able to forgive others the same way (Matt. 18:21 – 22). When Jesus taught his disciples how to pray, he included, "Forgive us our debts, as we also have forgiven our debtors" (Matt. 6:12). If we want to experience the kind of healing that comes from a "but God" encounter, then we must forgive. Forgiving others invites God's forgiveness and healing into our hearts. I knew that I would never be completely healed if I didn't forgive the woman who abused me.

In my junior year of college, I often hosted prayer meetings in my dorm room. These were great times of prayer, worship, and fellowship with other young men who were followers of Jesus. During this time, I realized that if I wanted to grow and become stronger in my faith, then I couldn't ignore any longer my need to forgive this woman. So I made the choice to forgive. While my painful emotions remained buried inside me until I later told

Tiffany, my fiancée, I had at least taken a huge step toward healing by making forgiveness a deliberate decision.

I need to clarify a crucial point. Forgiveness doesn't mean you have to be the person's best friend. Let me be clear: The woman who hurt me — we are not friends. I wasn't seeking any kind of relationship with her. She even tried to contact me on a few occasions after I became an adult, and I once took her call. Because I had forgiven her, I was able to be kind as well as clear. I have forgiven her, but forgiveness and restoration are not the same.

Forgiveness is what I like to call an "inside job." Only you can do it, from the inside out. Your heart has to make the leap of forgiveness, and you have to work through the hurt in order to get to the point of forgiveness. You can forgive someone whether or not they ask you to. This is a process you go through yourself, dealing with feelings and attitudes on the inside. It's your decision, not your offender's.

If you truly forgive someone, you can be kind and compassionate, and even extend God's love to that person. You can want what's best for the person who hurt you. Forgiveness means that you're no longer walking around with bitterness, hatred, or animosity in your heart toward the person who hurt you.

But restoration is an "outside job." This is the external interaction between you and your offender. If the relationship is restored, by definition it goes back to the way it was. The person regains your trust, your respect, and your admiration. While we're commanded to forgive others, the Bible does not tell us that we must resume that relationship as if nothing happened. Forgiveness does not automatically produce restoration. So if this misunderstanding on restoration has been holding you back from forgiving someone, don't let it anymore.

My relationship with my abuser has not been restored back to what it was before the abuse occurred. In other words, I'm not inviting her over to play with my kids! That's called being unwise, not forgiveness. But I have forgiven her. I've released it. I trust and pray that she has asked God to forgive her for those actions.

The alternative leaves us trapped in victimhood. When we choose not to forgive, we blame that person or that event for what's happening to us today. We don't take responsibility for what we can do and instead blame that person or event for the bad things that happen in our life.

But when we forgive, we remove the blame. We show mercy. We exonerate that person, and we let go of the blame, bitterness, and grudge we have been holding. This is real freedom! It is the chance to move forward and stop looking backward. "Forgetting what is behind and straining toward what is ahead, I press on toward the goal to win the prize for which God has called me heavenward in Christ Jesus" (Phil. 3:13 – 14).

Think about it this way. The windshield of a car is a lot bigger than the rearview mirror. When we stop looking at the past, our future gets larger, more expansive. We realize that looking over our shoulder makes it difficult to move forward. Once we forgive, we can let go of that past and have freedom to achieve the future God has in store for us.

Another step in my healing process was recognizing the side effects of the abuse I suffered.

Address the Side Effects

Not only does our pain linger, but it also produces ongoing side effects. We have broken hearts, weary spirits, and aching bodies. Pain can make it hard to trust again. It can result in bitterness, fear, insecurities, and bad attitudes. Most of these effects are the result of not wanting to get hurt again, so walls are constructed and defense mechanisms are put in place.

Remember, hurting people hurt other people. Even though you may have forgiven those people who hurt you, consequences remain. You still need to recognize that the restoration process requires time for your wounds to heal. When others betray us, hurt us, offend us, we're left with consequences that don't end even after we've forgiven them. Ninety-nine percent — okay, actually 100 percent — of people who are healed are still affected by their wounds in some way.

This has been true in my life. I see the world a little differently because of my experience. As much as I love people and want to trust them, I'm still cautious about who I allow around my kids. I'm super-careful about who watches them, who they're with, and where they are. Because of what happened to me, I realize another adult can look normal, have a good job, be in the church or on staff at school and still be someone who would prey on young kids, teenagers, or even other adults. Yes, I'm healed. But I'm also wiser and more protective of my own kids and others who may be as vulnerable as I was at a young age. From my own experience and after helping and interacting with other people who have been abused,

I believe it is important to understand the side effects of abuse.

When we have intimacy with God and choose to forgive, when we give the hurt, the pain, and the person who hurt us to God, he heals us. We not only grow wiser, but we live life with compassion, kindness, and a deep inner strength. We know God's peace, so there's no need to retaliate. Has this been the case in your life?

Or are you still living with the hurt? Even in the midst of healing, even after a "but God" encounter has started the process, you can still experience side effects. Don't let these side effects play tricks with your mind and cause you to think that you're not being healed or cause you to live under condemnation or think you're unworthy of God's love. Side effects are normal when you've been wounded deeply.

For instance, maybe a boyfriend once verbally and physically abused you. Unless you forgive him, you will likely remain fearful, defensive, angry, and hurt, and you will avoid anyone with a potential to hurt you. But when you let the healing power of God make you whole, you start reacting differently. The potential for bitterness, victimhood, rage, and retribution melts into forgiveness, compassion, and wisdom. You've forgiven him. You can handle it when you run into him. But you're still dealing with side effects. You're aware of being more cautious when going on a date or entering a new relationship, even a casual friendship. You're more aware of other people's words and body language and their response to conflict. You seem to share yourself in layers as you try to build a strong foundation of trust with this new person.

Again, this process takes time. Sometimes you have to forgive daily the people who hurt you, releasing the painful power their wound has had in your life. This requires faith in God's ability to deal with them as well as trust in his commitment to heal your brokenness. The scars may linger, but over time they will fade and serve as reminders of God's restorative power in your life.

Tell Someone

In order to experience all that God has for you, there's one more step that's key to walking in complete wholeness and freedom. After you've grown in your relationship with God and forgiven the people who hurt you, you need to share your experience with other people. Sounds simple, but when abuse, a deep wound, or some type of dysfunctional behavior causes chronic pain, telling someone about it can be the hardest thing to do. As Joyce Meyer explains, "All too often, these hurts are simply swept under a rug in an attempt to make them go away."[1] I know firsthand that hiding these emotions doesn't make them disappear!

So many people are afraid to tell because they are afraid of how others would respond if they knew. What if they think less of me? Blame me for the event? Misunderstand me? View me as damaged goods? So instead, they just sit on it, figuring if they ignore it and don't talk about it, the hurt may eventually fade away. They especially hide it from the very people — loving family, trusted friends, caring mentors, and compassionate pastors — who could help them the most.

Even after we've stopped stiff-arming God, we may continue to keep others at arm's length. But God often uses other people as a powerful part of our healing process. There's something about the prayers, support, and encouragement of other caring, trustworthy individuals that helps to heal our wounds. When I consider the impact others have on our healing, I'm reminded of the paralyzed man whose friends went to great lengths — or should I say heights — to bring him before Jesus.

> A few days later, when Jesus again entered Capernaum, the people heard that he had come home. They gathered in such large numbers that there was no room left, not even outside the door, and he preached the word to them. Some men came, bringing to him a paralyzed man, carried by four of them. Since they could not get him to Jesus because of the crowd, they made an opening in the roof above Jesus by digging through it and then lowered the mat the man was lying on. When Jesus saw their faith, he said to the paralyzed man, "Son, your sins are forgiven."
>
> MARK 2:1–5

This man relied on his friends so that he could literally drop in on Jesus while he was teaching there in Capernaum. Unable to walk or perhaps even move, this man had no way to forge a path through the overflowing crowd spilling out of the house. But his resourceful friends refused to let this barrier prevent them from bringing him before the Lord for healing. If this man had become withdrawn and slipped into depression and isolation, he would likely have stiff-armed his friends and resigned himself to his paralysis. But instead he shared his need with others who carried him to the place and to the Person who could heal him.

The Courage to Tell

For eight years, I carried around my secret. When God radically changed my life at age seventeen, I still had not told anyone about my emotional scarring. Even though I started preaching shortly after my salvation experience in the team locker room, I kept all my shameful feelings hidden away. When I got a Bible degree in my early twenties, I still hadn't told anyone my story.

Finally, though, I found the courage to tell someone — my soon-to-be wife, Tiffany. She and I met while attending Evangel University. By that time I had already decided that I wanted to preach and fulfill the calling God had placed on me. Tiffany was not only beautiful and sweet but also strong in her faith.

During the time we dated, my secret hovered in the back of my brain most of the time, always trying to sneak toward the front. I had always assumed I should probably tell the person I planned to marry about the abuse. But as it became clear that Tiffany and I were headed toward the altar, I was tempted to do the opposite. I told myself I could just deal with it. I told myself that it was no big deal and would never affect our relationship. Despite my rationalizations, I became determined to do the right thing and clue her in. Somehow deep down I knew that hiding keeps you from healing.

I'll never forget sitting in the driver's seat of my car,

gripping that steering wheel with sweaty palms and listening to my thumping heart, on my way to tell her. What if she saw me differently? What if she no longer loved me? The "what ifs" buzzed like flies around my mind. But I was able to go through with it because I didn't want to live a lie. I told her.

In a soft, compassionate voice, she replied, "I'm so sorry that happened to you." We just sat there together in the intimacy of a burden shared. She didn't press for more details, and I didn't give any. Simply by telling her, this huge weight was lifted from my shoulders. Her compassionate acceptance of me allowed me to take a huge step forward on my "but God" process of healing.

It brought great comfort just to have another Christian who knew and who was praying for me. I no longer had to carry this burden alone. Over the years of our marriage, I have shared more details and experienced more and more healing.

A few years ago, I was involved in a community group with some other guys. I shared my story with them, and as a result experienced a greater level of victory in my life. Another step forward in my healing. When we accept that incredible challenge of telling somebody, and then telling somebody else, and continuing on that journey, God uses our moments of openness to bring healing to our lives. Every time we share, we peel back another layer of our hiding place.

Recently, after years of avoiding it, I shared this story with my church. Would people still want to follow a pastor who had been abused? I didn't know the answer, but I also knew that I needed to tell them what had happened to me.

When we tell others our story, we are opening a door not to let the story out, but to let ourselves walk through that door toward freedom. Each time we share, that door gets opened a little wider. God's Word tells us, "Confess your faults one to another, and pray one for another, that ye may be healed. The effectual fervent prayer of a righteous man availeth much" (James 5:16 KJV). So often we think of confession as telling others what we have done wrong. But it also involves sharing the wrongs done to us and their impact. We open ourselves to more of God's healing and acceptance as we tell our secrets and share our burdens with other believers.

Please understand, however, that you must take great care in choosing the people whom you tell. Make sure it is someone you trust, someone who loves the Lord, someone who cares about you and your well-being. You may have been carrying around fig leaves for so long that you aren't sure who is the one you could tell. If so, I would encourage you to consider seeing a Christian counselor. A professional counselor could help you to work through the difficulty of talking about the abuse to begin the healing.

The Power to Change

Let God touch your life and heal you, and you will naturally want to help people who are struggling with similar wounds. Once you allow God into your pain, you discover how he can turn your mess into a message. According to Scripture, we were not created to be victims sidelined by our injuries. Instead, "in all these things we are more than conquerors through him who loved us" (Rom. 8:37). Notice, you're not just a conqueror—you're MORE than a conqueror!

Your past can't hold you down. Abuse can't hold you down. Betrayal can't hold you down. The family you were born into can't hold you down. Only you can hold you down—when you don't allow God to heal you and then free you from what you've been through.

God calls all of us to help the hurting and the lost. What is he calling you to do? Where do you feel a passion? You may not be a pastor or a minister in a church building, but you *are* a source of freedom wherever you are if you're healed from your pain and willing to use it for good. This is how God's strength is manifest through our weakness, how his grace spreads, every day, in places all around the world.

Listen, someone hurt you. That's a fact. And you have been carrying that hurt with you and struggling to get past it. That's a fact. But the truth is more powerful than those facts. The fact is that you went through something awful, but the truth is that you can move forward.

God can take bad situations, harmful scenarios, and huge hurts and transform them into something good—into your purpose, your passion, your power. Don't despair! God can take *any* situation and turn it into a *good* situation.

You're wounded ... but God heals you!

3

We're Insecure ...
But God Gives Us Confidence

I praise you because I am fearfully
and wonderfully made;
your works are wonderful,
I know that full well.

PSALM 139:14

Tiffany and I met at Evangel University when she was a freshman and I was a senior. It didn't take long for me to figure out that I could fall for this girl, that she resembled the kind of woman I wanted to marry. My future — our *shared* future — began to rush toward me when — enter, from stage right — my old friend, Insecurity.

I wasn't surprised. I had entertained thoughts of marriage before — could I be a good husband? Would I be able to have a successful marriage? Would my past experiences hinder me so much that I wouldn't be able to succeed with another person? After all, my parents had gotten divorced — was I destined to do the same?

Marriage wasn't my only worry. In most relationships, as two people are getting to know and to love each other, doubts begin to surface. The closer Tiffany and I became, the more my insecurities exploded with fears and doubts. When we strip away the layers and reveal who we really are, we often wonder if the other person can continue to accept us. Sure, Tiffany liked me when I was cool, confident, and ultra-Christian, but could she handle who I was when I was goofy, insecure, and a spiritual mess? The pattern usually involved my feelings of insecurity being trumped by God's presence and Tiffany's loving patience. In other words, our relationship became a series of "but God" moments. My insecurity would take me to the brink of believing that she could never know who I really am *and* love me. But God consistently took me over that cliff of fear as Tiffany surprised me by accepting and loving the real me.

Worlds Collide

My insecurities were compounded by the differences in our backgrounds; she and I brought two very different worlds colliding together. There was the issue of two races and two cultures along with two different lifestyles clashing and smashing as we tried to form something new. Her background was radically different from mine, almost the opposite. She lived part of her childhood in Grand Island, Nebraska, and the other part in Wisconsin. Small towns. Northern. White. She was from a Christian family, and her parents were not only still married: her dad was a *pastor*.

She invited me to come home with her over Christmas break that first year after we met. I accepted, excited at the thought of meeting the people who were responsible for who she was, but I also understandably was feeling a little anxious. It went beyond the normal questions of would they like me or would they approve of me.

You see, after Tiffany and I met in August and started to date, she wrote her parents a letter about me, telling them she had met a Christian guy, that he was a man of God who was already doing some preaching and was planning to go into full-time ministry. She painted a great picture of me, and I later found out that after reading it, her mother told her father, "I think Tiffany has met her husband!"

There's just one little detail she failed to include — can you guess which one? My optimistic, sweet, it's-all-good wife left out the color of my skin. Did she forget? Did she think it was irrelevant? It *was* irrelevant to us, but imagine the surprise her parents experienced when they showed up at the university later that fall to visit and met *me* for the first time!

We made it through that visit at the school just fine, but I knew that by the time we visited at Christmas, they would have had time to think through my relationship with their daughter. So I had a few more worries than normal, wondering if Tiffany's parents could indeed accept me as easily as she did.

It's not that they were unkind or aloof or anything. We were just so different. Tiffany's family went to church Sunday morning, Sunday night, and Wednesday night. And don't forget all of the special services throughout the year. She'd also go to the church during the week for things like worship practice or youth leadership team meetings. Sometimes she even took her dad's keys and unlocked the church building when needed.

After church services on Sunday nights, the family would go to Country Kitchen along with other people from the church to socialize, laugh, and talk. If it wasn't clear before, this visit made it crystal clear. Tiffany's life revolved around God, church, and family. This was her world.

When I visited her family, I was the only black person in the neighborhood. Okay, forget the 'hood — I might have been the only black person in town! Her family was always welcoming and warm, but it was different from what I was used to — very different. There were no loud, outrageous voices. No alcohol or cigarette smoke at the family party. No one dropping an "F" bomb, no one acting like a fool in the living room, no one about to explode into an angry rant. Most confusing of all, there was no Luther Vandross or Marvin Gaye playing in the background! How can you call it a real family gathering without a little Luther?

All joking aside, I experienced some major culture shock.

Guess Who's Coming to Dinner

But that was my visit to *her* home. Her visit to *my* house was a different story. Because of my parents' divorce and some of the dysfunctional history there, Tiffany and I were engaged by the time I dared to take her home. She had a ring on her finger, but I was nervous (another word I used for insecure) about bringing this somewhat sheltered, northern, lily-white, small-town preacher's daughter into my past in Wewoka.

As I pulled the car up to my dad's house for the very first time with Tiffany, I wondered if she'd still keep that ring on her finger after she experienced "Little Chicago," as Paul Harvey once described Wewoka because of its prevalent problems with drugs and violence. Would she be able to see beyond my dysfunctional family and recognize a future for us?

We got out of the car and immediately my dad was there, welcoming my fiancée. "Heeey! It's so good to have you here!"

Uh-oh.

"So good to have you!"

He was laying it on thick.

"I made a special dinner for us tonight!"

As he ushered us in, it became obvious my dad was whippin' out a *spread* for my fiancée, one he'd been planning for days. I peeked at Tiffany out of the corner of my eye. As always, she just had a big smile on her face. So far, so good.

My dad ushered us over to the grill, which was already lit and smoking in the backyard. Clearly, he was excited and a little proud to be treating our special guest to some top-notch food for dinner. Smiling, he opened the lid, and there on the grill was ... a raccoon!

I am not kidding you.

My dad had outdone himself.

There by my side stood a lovely young woman who had been raised on pot roast and mashed potatoes, maybe some fried chicken from time to time, and prime rib at Christmas. I, on the other hand, grew up eating 'coon, rabbit, squirrel, deer, pheasant, duck, quail, pig's feet, pig's ears, cow liver, chitterlings, hog-head cheese, and the occasional road kill. (Okay, my apologies — I know I'm making you hungry. If you need to go grab a snack, I understand.) For Tiffany's first visit to my unique world, my dad had offered only the best: fresh raccoon with its head still on!

Tiffany's world and my world were crashing into each other at warp speed. I was so worried about what was going through her head. But I tried to play it cool and half-jokingly asked, "Hey! We're still getting married, though, right?"

Questions Become Doubts

Have you ever been in a situation in which your seeds of insecurity not only took root but began producing a bumper crop of sour fruit? Maybe, like me, you struggled to feel like you could reconcile your vast differences with someone in a special relationship. Or perhaps you were promoted into a position for which you secretly felt unqualified and unprepared. Or a series of disappointments left you questioning your abilities as a parent.

Whatever the context, most people battle certain personal insecurities in their lives. But the battle is not the problem — it's giving in without a fight or resigning yourself to losing that's the problem. Looking back at my relationship with Tiffany, I discovered that these battles with self-doubt and insecurity can become opportunities for some incredible "but God" encounters.

But these battles weren't easy. My relational insecurity went beyond my perception of what Tiffany thought. I began to imagine what our future together might look like, and it was enough to make me pause. Back on campus, I went to a professor I liked and trusted, hoping to either set my mind at ease or have my fears confirmed. I laid out my list of questions: If Tiffany and I got married, would we be accepted? Could we have an interracial marriage and a successful ministry at the same time? And what about our future kids? What kinds of struggles might they face?

My wise and compassionate professor listened intently. While he had no problem with interracial marriage, he knew that some people did. He was honest and told me we would likely have struggles being accepted. He suspected my ministry might be affected.

I felt the pieces of our two worlds shattering and falling around me. Felt more insecure about whether we could successfully build a new world, a committed and godly marriage, one that could withstand any of the challenges that arose from being together.

And it didn't take long to face that first challenge.

Tiffany and I received a letter from one of her extended family members, someone she liked and trusted, a person she respected and valued. This relative wrote to express concern about our relationship; according to this person, we could not have a biblical marriage because of our different races.

I didn't need to consult a theologian to know that I didn't agree with this opinion, but I was insecure, and this made me think long and hard and second-guess my proposal. There was no doubt that I loved Tiffany and she loved me. But was that enough? And even if God blessed our union, and I believed he would, could we withstand people like her family member who had written the letter?

Some days it was all I could do to not convince myself that Tiffany would be better off without me. But God was faithful, and his truth began to pierce through my insecurities with "but God" reminders of his strength, power, and purpose for my life. Sometimes I experienced these "but God" moments as I prayed about my relationship with Tiffany. Other times, her unconditionally loving acceptance of me reflected our Father's love in a way that I could not deny.

In addition to these "but God" moments that propelled our relationship forward, we also saw his hand remove potential obstacles to our union. For instance, the family member who sent the letter warning us against marrying changed her stance. She again explored what the Bible had to say and ended up giving us her blessing before the wedding. Tiffany came to Wewoka again, this time for Thanksgiving dinner *after* we were married. She did great with the yams and collard greens, but she had to draw the line at the chitlins after I finally told her what they were made of.

My journey to confidence has been and continues to be a process. Obviously, Tiffany and I went through with the marriage, the ministry, and having kids, and I thank God that all three are thriving. But if it had not been for the many "but God" moments along the way, I doubt I would have been able to push through my insecurities to embrace what God had for me.

If I had tried to please everyone else and done what they wanted me to do, I wouldn't have pursued our relationship and married Tiffany. I would have missed out on the best thing that's ever happened to me besides my relationship with Jesus. Tiffany is the BBQ sauce on my ribs, the jelly on my toast, the gravy on my biscuits, the butter on my popcorn, the hot sauce on my chitterlings. She makes me want to shout!

Do We Have What It Takes?

My relationship with Tiffany is not the only arena in which "but God" moments have defeated my insecurities. When we started People's Church twelve years ago, I became more aware of my personality type. Before this I had been traveling and preaching at various places, which was fine. But now settling in one spot would require a different approach to relationship — sustained relationship — which would require time with people on a recurring basis. I began to second-guess myself.

If I was going to be a great pastor, then I couldn't be an introvert, or so I thought at the time. Shouldn't a great pastor be more of a people person? Shouldn't he be running meetings all day? Shouldn't he be visiting the sick, evangelizing in every neighborhood, and forming some neighborhood committees? Shouldn't he be out fishing, hunting, golfing, and having meals with people every day? I didn't like myself and couldn't understand why God made me the way I am and then called me to do what I was doing. I knew he hadn't made a mistake, but I just couldn't figure out what was going on.

Maybe you are dealing with a similar issue. You're having a hard time liking yourself because of some significant insecurities. The truth is that we all deal with insecurities at certain points in our lives. We sometimes say things like "he or she is so insecure" as if it's a weakness the person could easily correct but chooses to ignore.

The bottom line is that insecurity isn't fun. We can often trace its cause back to some painful event in the past. And though we desperately want to, ridding ourselves of insecurity is just not easy. In fact, the majority of us struggle with insecurity in not one, but many areas. We wonder if we have what it takes, if we can bring enough to the game, if we can be who God really wants us to be.

The Comparison Trap

One of the biggest reasons I questioned whether I could be a good pastor was because I compared myself to other people, especially other pastors. Most of the pastors I knew and admired were enormous extroverts. They not only *wanted* to be around people all the time; they seemed to like it and be energized by it. Whenever I compared myself to them and came up short, I would pray for God to change me into what I assumed I should be — someone just like those guys.

It got to the point where I would look at myself and analyze the way I felt about being around people. When I looked at some of these other pastors and considered how they seemed to feel, I'd see how different they were. And I would see myself as a loser. That's insecurity. It talks like that. It focuses on our weaknesses and fears. And it was talking to me and messing up my self-worth. I was feeling like a failure, an inferior version of what I should be.

Over the years, I've realized that I'm not the only one struggling with insecurity because of how I see myself compared to others. Comparing ourselves to other people is a dangerous game that we were never meant to play. Comparison is the quickest way to find yourself unhappy with who you are or what you have. Look at the guy at work who is good at putting words together and find yourself feeling less professional. Look for other moms going on field trips when you're heading off to your job, then criticize yourself for being a too-busy working parent. Notice that cute, fit woman with the great hair at the gym and wonder why you can't look as good as she does.

When we scroll through a social media page, we see the highlights of what everyone else is doing. Frequently, we are scrolling through those highlights while we are bored, maybe alone, maybe wishing our lives were a little different, if not like their lives seem to be on Instagram. We compare another person's exciting trip to the beach with the fact that we're still sitting here on the couch. Or working so many hours to make ends meet. We forget that Jane posts when she is experiencing a highlight, or when Bob landed that new account, not while they're sitting on the couch like you are. We compare our marriage to the Millers' as they Instagram a photo of their date night — and then we wonder what's wrong with our own.

We compare our inside self, the weaknesses we're all too familiar with, to another person's shiny, best-foot-forward outside package. We start looking down on ourselves, wondering why we are not like that other person. We wonder what's wrong with us. We overlook the fact that those better-than-us people have weaknesses and problems too, even if we can't spot them. They don't shout their weaknesses, their failures on Facebook or Twitter, but they're there. We never get the full story. Believe me, *no one* is exempt from insecurity. Throughout our lives, we all need "but God" encounters to break through these massive feelings of failure and to remind us of what's true.

You Talking to Me?

With reality TV, social media, and constant consumer reminders of what we need but don't have, we may have more fuel poured on the flame of our insecurity today, but the problem is not new. As we see in the Bible, people have had insecurities for thousands of years. Moses never had the Internet, and yet he struggled with doubts about who he was and what God was calling him to do.

When Moses was just a baby, Pharaoh passed an edict that all Hebrew boy babies be killed. But God intervened, and Moses' life was spared. This evidence shouts that

God had a purpose for Moses from the very beginning. But years later, Moses did not see himself the way God saw him. When God gave Moses specific instructions to lead the Israelites out of Egypt, Moses did not believe that he could do the job. He argued with God on three fronts, all focusing on his weaknesses: (1) Why choose me? ("Who am I that I should go to Pharaoh and bring the Israelites out of Egypt?" Ex. 3:11); (2) What if I'm not good enough? ("What if they do not believe me?" Ex. 4:1); and (3) What about my obvious flaws? ("I am slow of speech and tongue," Ex. 4:10). When these excuses didn't work, Moses tried begging God, "Please send someone else" (Ex. 4:13).

Think about this situation. Moses had God himself giving him instructions and commands of what to do, and he still doubted that he could succeed! Moses made the mistake of looking at himself through his own eyes. He remained insecure because he focused on what he *didn't* have and what he *wasn't* able to do. He saw himself as someone who couldn't put his words together, who couldn't stop stuttering, and who therefore couldn't lead and inspire confidence in others.

Moses' story reminds me of Romans 9:20, which says, "Shall what is formed say to the one who formed it, 'Why did you make me like this?'" This is a question we ask when we look at ourselves from our own limited perspective. We look around us and see what other people have. Then we look back at ourselves and feel inferior.

Just like Moses, when we focus only on our weaknesses, we end up forgetting that we have strengths — strengths that God gave us. Moses believed his greatest talent was running away from trouble. When he was younger, he had messed up big time. He had even murdered a man. He had been on the back side of the desert tending sheep for forty years and felt like a nobody. When he compared his shortcomings to the strengths of his brother Aaron, Moses felt certain he didn't have what it would take to do what God was telling him to do.

But God wasn't about to let Moses off the hook. You see, when God looked at the man he'd chosen, he didn't pay attention to all the weaknesses Moses had mentioned. God saw a leader. He saw someone with the fortitude to lead the people of God to their future home. Moses' "but God" encounter was basically an argument with God — and we all know how those tend to go!

Everything changed during Moses' "but God" encounter at that burning bush. God used him despite his insecurities and perceived weaknesses. Moses would have hidden behind his insecurities and lived a different life, but God showed him the great plan he had for his life.

God wants to do the same for you. God asks you to trust him to help you accomplish great feats that you could never achieve on your own. You may feel unsuccessful because you see yourself as different from those you admire. But the way you are is not by accident. It is on purpose. Follow God's leading and chase how he sees you — the original, authentic you, not the one you see only in brief glimpses.

Seeing Clearly

And how does God see you? The psalmist wrote, "I praise you because I am fearfully and wonderfully made; your works are wonderful, I know that full well" (Ps. 139:14). The same Creator of the heavens and the earth is the one who created you, just as you are. You have a purpose to carry out with the abilities and traits you have been given.

The powerful truth of God's Word brought about a "but God" moment and helped me overcome my insecurities. Sure, I had known the Scripture in my head for years, but one day while meditating on it, I had a "but God" encounter that began to change the way I viewed myself. In that moment, God was speaking directly to me about my identity. In response, I made the decision to embrace what it meant and let it sink into my heart, and it began to change the way I looked at myself and how I acted. This "but God" experience had an immediate impact on my view of myself, but this "but God" transformation was also a process. When feelings of self-doubt would creep in, I would remember the psalmist's words and trust who God says I am, not my temporary emotions.

As I meditated on what God said in the Bible about me, God began to transform my insecurities. I began to believe that God had made me "fearfully and wonderfully." I started to grasp that the kind of husband I would be was uniquely me, and that my past did not need to dictate how I would treat Tiffany. Just because my parents divorced didn't mean that my marriage would be doomed to fail. Just because I had been abused didn't mean that I couldn't be in a healthy relationship. God made me unique, and he made me to be the kind of man who loved Tiffany enough to be her husband. And after sixteen years of marriage, he's still making me into the husband he wants me to be.

I had to go through a similar process in order to gain confidence in my ability to be a good pastor, despite being an introvert. Gradually, the truth began to sink in. God fearfully and wonderfully made me this way. I've always been an introvert. I'm wired this way. God doesn't see my introversion as a weakness. He's not comparing me to Rick Warren or Joyce Meyer or T. D. Jakes. He had a deliberate and special purpose in mind when he called me to pastor to so many people in the Oklahoma City area.

I began to let go of my insecurity about my personality and to embrace that I was made that way by my Creator — for a reason. I think Paul had this in mind when he wrote his letter to the church at Rome: "Just as our bodies have many parts and each part has a special function, so it is with Christ's body. We are all parts of his one body, and each of us has different work to do. And since we are all one body in Christ, we belong to each other, and each of us needs all the others" (Rom. 12:4 – 5 NLT). We have been designed the way we are as a part to contribute to the whole — God's wonderful church, the body of Christ.

The church is made up of many parts — MANY parts! Not all the same parts; we are all different. God likes it this way. He made us that way: one body (Christ's body), and we all belong to each other to function as a whole. In fact, our weaknesses help us to see that we need each other.

As Paul continued his letter to the Roman church, he explained, "God has given each of us the ability to do certain things well" (Rom. 12:6 NLT). He then cataloged a variety of abilities and gifts — prophecy, service, teaching, encouragement, generosity, leadership, kindness — and once again reinforces that our inter-dependence is part of God's original plan.

God has given us different gifts. We didn't choose our gifts. Our parents didn't give us our gifts. God did! He has given us certain talents, strengths, abilities, and personalities to do certain things well. You don't do everything well; if you think you do, your parents or your friends are lying to you. Yes, you do certain things well. So what is it that you do best? What do you recognize in yourself? And even more, what do others whom you trust see in you? Where do you have the most value? Embrace that gift!

Learning My Strengths

Meditating on and embracing God's Word adjusted my perspective. I realized that I needed to figure out what my gift was and to use it effectively, instead of focusing on what I saw as potential weaknesses. I had to trust God's timeless, unshakable truth instead of the roller coaster of my temporary feelings.

As I studied God's Word, I began to see I had the gift of teaching. What a relief the first time I realized my gifting was in an area I was already passionate about. Ephesians 4:11 – 12 resonated with me: "And He gave some as apostles, and some as prophets, and some as evangelists, and some as pastors and teachers, for the equipping of the saints for the work of service, to the building up of the body of Christ" (NASB). God made me a teacher; I had found my part! I had been trying to be a left foot when I was really a right hand. I was doing the job of the right hand but trying to fit into the left shoe. And that wasn't helping anyone.

Another thing I had to do was realize where I added the most value. I love to talk finances and get into the nitty-gritty of the budget, but that is not where I add the most value to my church. My strength is in vision casting and leading and teaching. These are my sweet spots. I need to use my time wisely on those things and allow other people to use their gifts to accomplish the other things so they can be fulfilled by doing their part in the body of Christ.

Again, this journey has not been a quick one. When I was struggling with feeling like my introversion was a hurdle, I kept thinking I needed to be a certain way to be "right." That caused me to think other people needed to be a certain way. I thought Tiffany should pay the bills like I did. I thought my worship pastor should have a thick skin like I do. Even though I wasn't happy with myself, I expected other people to be like me. If they weren't, I felt they were wrong. But when I realized that I am fearfully and wonderfully made, I began to see that God doesn't *tolerate* my personality; he *celebrates* it! I learned to celebrate me and then to celebrate other people. This was a significant turning point for me personally and for People's Church.

I looked around and realized that being the right hand fit in well with another pastor on staff who was the proverbial left foot. He was an extrovert who enjoyed being around other people and counseling them. (Now, if I did counseling all the time, I would probably need a little counseling myself. Right hand.) That was his sweet spot. He was the perfect complement to who I was and the jobs I needed to do. And I became secure enough to let him handle his area while I worked in mine: "Let everyone be sure that he is doing his very best, for then he will have the personal satisfaction of work well done and won't need to compare himself with someone else" (Gal. 6:4 TLB). How freeing it was to realize what *my* job was and to go after it with everything I had.

Don't miss out on what God has for you because of your insecurities. Ask him to show you that you are fearfully and wonderfully made, and show you your sweet spot. Discover who you are through God's eyes. Trust the truth of his character and the promises in his Word instead of your feelings, questions, doubts, and fears that wash over you from time to time. Your perception is limited, inaccurate, and biased by present events. God's view is timeless, perfect, and unlimited by circumstances.

One of the most debilitating things we can do is limit our potential by relying only on our perception of who we are. We were meant to rely on God's power to use us in ways beyond our imagination, ways that will turn our weaknesses inside out, move us beyond our comfort zones, and transform our understanding of who we are.

You are one part of a body, a piece of the puzzle that is *essential* to making the whole thing work. See yourself as God sees you, because your own vision is too limited, your eyes too small to see the truth. You are fearfully and wonderfully made. Once you grow in your faith and begin to trust God's truth, you will realize that you are so much stronger, gifted, and equipped than you ever realized. We get stuck in temporary hindrances and feel insecure — but God reminds us of the truth!

4

We Search for Identity ...
But God Gives Us Purpose

*"For those who exalt themselves will be humbled,
and those who humble themselves will be exalted."*

MATTHEW 23:12

The summer before my senior year of college, I was invited to preach in a church in New York. Still new to traveling and speaking, I was already nervous, but to add another complication, my current crush — someone I pursued before meeting Tiffany — belonged to this same church. She would be there, her parents would be there, and while I wanted to preach God's Word and minister to the congregation, a part of me wanted only to impress this girl and her family.

I was still working on my preaching style and had

tried on a few different ones. I went through a brief Southern preacher phase ("I'm here-uh today-ah, to tell you-ah, about God's plan-ah!"). Some black preachers even like to add an extra vowel at the end of phrases for an extra "ah" effect. Trust me, *only* try this inside your own home. I also flirted with the idea of having an organ playing behind me — along with an occasional bass line to really get them going wild. I considered anything that seemed effective or memorable as a viable option for my preaching.

This time, on my way to New York, I just knew I was on to something. For a sophisticated, urban church, I'd take a high-road approach and drop some Greek on them.

Yes, you already know how this went over.

But I had good intentions. See, I knew this preacher back in Oklahoma who knew how to get it done on Sunday. He would take a verse, go back to the Greek origin of the key words, dissect them, shed new light on their application, and have people crying in the aisles, his sermon was so good. Seriously, this style *worked* for this dude.

And I *knew* I could make this work for me. People would see my knowledge of the ancient Greek text from the Bible, and my girlfriend's dad would probably start calling me "son" right after I got done preaching. The mom would start knitting my Christmas stocking with "Herbert" across the front. This girl and her family would realize my godliness along with my intelligence with all the Greek that I would rattle off. It was a winning plan. I knew it.

Sunday arrived. These days I wear jeans when I preach,

but this was back in the days when you *had* to put on a suit and tie for church if you wanted to be taken seriously. So I had on my three-piece and shiny black shoes, and I strode to the pulpit carrying my huge Bible under my arm with my notes bulging out its sides. I looked like a preacher was supposed to look.

Gazing across that auditorium, I spotted my special girl sitting with her parents, or, as I thought of them, my future in-laws. So I opened my Bible, started speaking, and all those Greek notes began staring up at me. Before long I began sprinkling them into my sermon. I read words from Scripture, provided the original Greek (usually uncertain about proper pronunciation, but I didn't let that slow me down), and tried to sound like I knew what I was talking about.

It bombed.

I mean *really* bombed. Have you ever had one of those out-of-body experiences where you hear yourself talking, and all you're thinking is, *Somebody stop me!* But when you're preaching, you can't. So I didn't. And it got progressively worse. There were words coming out of my mouth, but I was thinking, *What am I doing? There go all my future Christmases with the girl of my dreams! How can I turn this around?*

But it was too late.

Finally, church ended, and I was hoping for just a little encouragement, you know, that it wasn't as bad as I thought. But it was. Polite, cool small talk followed, about anything except my sermon. To make matters worse, I had to go to lunch with my former would-be girlfriend and her parents. *How could this have happened?* I thought

I had a home-run sermon, but I struck out before the bat ever left my shoulder.

Looking back, I know why it failed ... I had copied and pasted someone else's version of success onto myself. I was searching for who I was, and I learned the hard way that this wasn't it.

I eventually found my way into my own style of preaching — one that no one else would be able to duplicate, one that was all mine. I could have been a second-rate version of someone else, but God helped me to be the first-rate version of me. I began to trust that God knew what he was doing. It took a lot of practice, experience, and soul-searching. And it finally took a willingness to allow God to work in my life for me to realize that I needed to work on being the best Herbert Cooper, not a caricature of some other preacher. This was another "but God" transformation that took a little time for me to grow into.

Yes, it was slow going. I can remember plenty of other times when I tried something that didn't work. But I also remember being in the middle of some sermons, trying something, and thinking, *Ooh! That worked! This is good. This is me.* I would try it again to make sure. And God was confirming in my heart that this was me. He was truly helping me discover my own personal style, which was exhilarating. God helped me accept what *I* did well.

When You Grow Up

Can you relate? Do you ever feel like even though you're an adult, you're still trying to figure out what you're going to be when you grow up? We're expected to have our lives figured out by the time we're adults, but the truth is that many of us find ourselves figuring out who we are throughout our lives. We chase after things that we hope will make us successful, which in turn will prove we're significant and worthy people. Unfortunately, they don't.

Or maybe you felt you discovered early in life who you really are. You were scaling milestones when life suddenly threw you a curveball. The dreams you thought you had figured out got blurred by the circumstances of life. Now you're at a crossroads you never expected to face.

Life can change directions on a dime. Overnight, your company can downsize, and you find out that you're losing your job. In a few sentences, you can learn that your spouse is having an affair or that you can't bear children. Relationships, circumstances, and possessions that seemed permanent disappear in the blink of an eye. Just like that. You find yourself in an identity crisis you never saw coming. But these changes can become platforms for new dreams. What can seem like the end can end up being a new beginning with God.

No matter what you're facing in life, whether you're trying to figure out who you are and how you fit into life for the first time or the twentieth time, or you're in one of those crossroads where your identity is being tested, you can rely on God to show you who he made you to be. Through "but God" encounters, you can discover who you are. While there's no magic formula for making these moments happen, I want to share with you five thought-provoking questions that have helped me experience a number of "but God" revelations and discover my true purpose-filled identity.

What Do You Dream About?

We've all known daydreamers. In elementary school, they were the kids who seemed to be looking out the window, thinking about far-away things, but definitely not the lesson being taught. What were they thinking about? Hitting a home run at the next Little League game? Making a bunch of money with a lemonade stand? Maybe they dreamed about going to Disney World instead of school. Daydreams are things that *could* happen but probably won't. And then there's the pipe dream, something that's just never going to happen no matter how much energy you pour into it. Envision this with me: *There are five seconds left in the fourth quarter of the NBA finals, and Kevin Durant passes me the ball. I dribble down court; the crowd is screaming at the top of their lungs! They count down, "5 ... 4 ... 3 ... 2 ... 1" and the announcer blares, "Herbert Cooper with the fade away jumper!" Swish! Nothing but net. We won! We won! We won the NBA championship!*

Okay, that's a pipe dream. The chances of it happening — nil. Let's just say I'm enjoying that pipe dream while my kids are still shorter than I am. I bring my dream to life as I play basketball with my kids. They range in age from nine down to five, and let me tell you, I *own* them! I block their shots. I score at will. There's no mercy from this dad! I will win while I still can!

If you share this kind of dream, you know what I'm talking about. Realistically, you know that your age, height, weight, and experience are not magically going to change overnight so that you wake up looking and playing like Lebron. Yes, we experience all kinds of different dreams. But in the end, actualizing our dream boils down to knowing if it's a dream from God or just a flight of fancy.

One of the Bible's most famous dreamers was Joseph. His brothers sold him into slavery, and in case you didn't hear this story in Sunday school (or see the amazing Technicolor musical), here's how it goes. His father, Jacob (also called Israel), had a total of twelve sons, but Jacob "loved Joseph more than any of his other sons" (Gen. 37:3). Joseph's brothers all knew this, and as might be expected, they weren't too thrilled with that favoritism.

Jealous brothers and the "coat of many colors" usually come to mind when we think of Joseph, but let's not forget that he had a few dreams of his own. And Joseph didn't have just any dream. He didn't have a pipe dream that was never going to happen or a daydream or a scary dream. He had a God-given dream for his life.

Near the beginning of his story in Genesis 37, we read that "Joseph had a dream" (v. 5) about his sheaf of wheat standing upright while his brothers' sheaves bowed down to it. He shared this dream with his brothers, much to their annoyance. Then he had another dream. In the second, the sun, moon, and eleven stars bowed down to him.

Now, I don't know about you, but if I had a couple dreams where things were bowing down to me, I probably wouldn't go tell those "things" about it. But good ole Joseph, this seventeen-year-old, has such zeal for his dreams that he describes them to the people closest to him: his brothers and his father. His brothers did not share his enthusiasm. We can imagine how preposterous the dreams must have seemed to them — one brother talking about how when they were all working in the field, tying bunches of grain, his sheaf of grain stood upright, and the sheaves of his brothers bowed down to it. His older brothers asked if they would have to submit to their younger brother. *Right.*

When he told his father, Jacob, about a second dream, even Jacob was appalled: "Will your mother and I and your brothers actually come and bow down to the ground before you?" (Gen. 37:10). Jacob reprimanded Joseph for his dream, but the Bible says he "kept the matter in mind" (v. 11). Maybe he wondered if there was something to the dreams after all.

Joseph's jealous brothers finally had enough of him and his big dreams. So they sold him to some merchants, slave traders, passing by in a caravan. Then they covered his richly ornamented robe in goat's blood to convince Jacob that his beloved son was dead. The future suddenly didn't look so bright for Joseph. Life had been good until he shared his dreams and pushed his brothers to their breaking point.

So what about his dream? Was it just a fantasy, a pipe dream after all? No, Joseph's dream held real power because it was from God. When we experience that kind of revelation, we must cling to it regardless of how our lives may change.

I relate to Joseph's story. One day when I was seventeen years old, I was supposed to be mowing the grass. There were two tall hedges, one on each side of the steps leading to the front porch. Leaving the motor running, I stopped pushing the mower and made my way up the stairs. I stood in between those hedges and, instead of mowing, I dreamed I was preaching to the tall grass I was supposed to be mowing. I envisioned the blades of grass as thousands of people.

I had been a Christian for only a short time, and that daydream was powerful to me. Tears filled my eyes and started rolling down my cheeks. Crazy, isn't it? This little country boy from Wewoka, Oklahoma, was dreaming big dreams. I even envisioned giving an altar call to those blades of grass and the grass coming forward to make a decision for Christ!

Little did I know that in my early twenties I would travel across America and then to Africa, preaching before thousands of people. I had no idea back then that by the age of twenty-six I would start a church and minister to many more thousands. And as much as I'd like to say the path has been smooth from porch to pulpit, the truth is that I've had to learn a lot — about myself, my talents, and where they intersect with God's purpose for my life. If I had told most people about my dream of preaching to thousands, it would have sounded crazy or, at best, been written off as "cute." But God had given me that dream, and it was powerful for me. He gave me a glimpse of my future purpose, and I saw it. I believed it!

God gives us dreams. In the book of Acts, we're told that "old men will dream dreams" (2:17). We're shown examples of dreams God has given people throughout Scripture, including Joseph, Job, Solomon, Samuel, Jacob, Joseph the husband of Mary, John, and Paul. What do you dream about? What are the things that are on your heart? What are the things that you envision for your life?

If you didn't have to worry about working a job that paid the bills — if money were no object — what would you want to do for the rest of your life? That truly is the ten-million-dollar question. This question may spark the dreams you've never allowed yourself to put into words or share with others. It's ultimately not about money but about revealing the thing God wired you to do.

To find out who you are, you have to find the God-inspired dream for your life.

Don't be afraid to start dreaming.

What Are You Good At?

It's important to have a God-inspired dream, but sometimes it can be difficult to distinguish between a daydream, a pipe dream, or a God-inspired dream. One of the ways I've learned to determine if my dream is from God is by asking the question, Am I good at what I'm dreaming about?

We've all seen talent contest shows like *American Idol* where a contestant believes they sound awesome and auditions. With unassailable confidence, they take the stage, open their mouth, and ... the sound is horrible. Screeching cats, scraping chalkboard, and high-pitched cartoon character voices all combined. It might make for huge TV ratings, but apparently many of these contestants haven't encountered the cold hard truth of their vocal limitations. They've got a dream but no talent.

It's frustrating to have a huge dream but not the ability to achieve that dream. Pipe dreams will frustrate you. So it becomes important to take an honest look at what you're good at. Taking that candid look at your abilities is not easy, but it's freeing to discover how God made you and what he made you for.

Since we've been talking about Joseph, let's ask this question of him. How did his dreams for his life match up with what he was good at?

After Joseph's brothers sold him, he ended up in Egypt, working at the house of Potiphar, the captain of the guard for the pharaoh of Egypt. This could have ended up being merely a way for Joseph to survive, but God had other plans for him. We're told, "The LORD gave him success in everything he did" (Gen. 39:3). Potiphar put Joseph in charge of his entire household and everything he owned.

Joseph's success was short-lived. Mrs. Potiphar tried to seduce him, and after he fled, she told her husband that Joseph had tried to seduce her. Potiphar put Joseph in prison, where the warden put him in charge of the other inmates. The Lord once again "gave him success in whatever he did" (Gen. 39:23). The warden didn't have to think about anything under Joseph's care.

Finally, Pharaoh noticed Joseph's talents and placed him in charge of the palace and eventually all of Egypt. This went on for years and years, and Joseph had incredible success in this position.

Clearly, Joseph was an exceptional leader. His talents and gifts matched up with the dream he had about being a leader way back when he was only seventeen. Each new role allowed him to develop and hone his gift just a little bit more, calling forth more of what God had placed in him. By the time Pharaoh recognized Joseph's talents, the dreamer had become a full-fledged leader. He had cultivated the talent he had been given.

Not long after my dream of preaching to thousands, I went away to college and received numerous opportunities to preach. Through these "but God" moments, I realized that I had some oratory skills and that God might be calling me to preach. God kept confirming this notion by providing new opportunities to develop and hone my preaching skills. Take a minute and think about the talents God has given you. You may have some things you "used to be good at" that you've put away because you think they have no value in your life anymore. You might have stopped using your strongest gifts because your current career doesn't afford you the opportunity, so you put those gifts on the shelf. But God keeps bringing up opportunities where your gifts come to mind or, better yet, must be utilized. Recognizing the pattern of your gifts and talents can confirm your true God-given identity and purpose. Just like Joseph, we all have areas where our dreams and our gifts will align to accomplish great things for God's glory.

What Do Others Say You're Good At?

Sometimes it can be difficult to know whether you're truly good at something unless you get some feedback that you're going in the right direction.

While I never had anyone tell me they were impressed with my knowledge of Greek, I did receive validation on my preaching. After I preached my first sermon to my high school youth group, my youth pastor encouraged me. During my sophomore year at college, the campus pastor and the president of the university made it possible for me to preach at chapel, which was particularly affirming.

Please understand that validation is not the same thing as approval. We just covered insecurities and comparing ourselves to others in the previous chapter; looking for approval from other people can quickly create and compound our insecurities. However, validation from a trusted source can let you know that you are not just reaching for a pipe dream, but that you're actually pursuing your God-given purpose.

God used the encouragement and opportunities I received to convince me that maybe I had something here. Maybe I could do this. Maybe preaching was what I was meant to do.

When we look at Joseph's life, it's easy to see that others saw what his gifts were. He kept getting "promoted," so to speak, because each man who was in charge of him saw incredible leadership skills. Potiphar saw that Joseph was great at organizing and managing, and he wanted Joseph to run his household and everything else he owned. The same thing happened when Joseph was in prison. The warden noticed Joseph and perhaps thought, *What in the world? The floors are clean, everything is in check, the guys are in line!* He saw that Joseph could not only keep things organized and in line, but people too. Then when Joseph interpreted Pharaoh's dream and told him it meant that Egypt would undergo seven years of plenty followed by seven years of famine, and he described what should be done to avoid disaster during the famine, Pharaoh couldn't think of anyone better to carry out the solution than Joseph himself. Joseph went from managing Potiphar's household and properties to managing an entire country (consider reviewing Joseph's story in Gen. 37 – 50). His dreams at the age of seventeen eventually were realized. No matter how harsh his circumstances, his God-given talents rose to the surface and were recognized. Joseph saved the land of Egypt from complete ruin during the seven-year famine because of his incredibly wise plan. Through a number of strategic decisions, he saved the nation as well as his own family.

Joseph's dreams lined up with his talents and with what others said he was good at. God was in charge, and God blessed everything he did!

What are others telling you? What is it that others tell you you're good at, even if that surprises you? Having mentors, close friends, coworkers, and spiritual leaders affirm your talents can not only save you from a misguided *American Idol* tryout but can also put you on the fast track to discover your talents and accomplish your God-given purpose.

What Are You Passionate About?

Each time one of these powerful men wanted to put Joseph in a major leadership role, he grabbed the bull by the horns and went for it. Joseph got things done. He never said, "Nah, I'll pass. I'd rather just do what I'm doing." He was better than anyone else they could find to troubleshoot and solve problems.

He loved organizing Potiphar's household, getting it to run smoothly. He did such a great job and was so passionate about it that Potiphar told him, "Man, I'm not concerned about anything in this house except my wife. You look after everything else. Pay my bills, watch my kids, make sure the animals are great. Take care of the other servants. You got this! Joseph, you are awesome, man! I've never seen anybody like you!" Joseph's passion for leadership was evident in how he handled every position he was given. He loved running the prison. And he excelled at running all of Egypt.

It may seem to be a cliché for a pastor to say that he's passionate about reaching people who are far from God, but that is where my heart is. I am passionate about doing whatever it takes to help that one person who hasn't heard about Jesus yet get the message. I am passionate about helping people do what they need to do so that they can understand who the Savior is and know him. I am passionate about seeing people grow in their faith. I try to achieve these things in many ways, but first and foremost is in my preaching every Sunday.

God gives us dreams. He gives us passions. No matter what season of life you're in, God can do great work through you. He can give you more "but God" moments.

What Moves You to Action?

What makes us angry, what stirs our spirit, and what pushes our buttons may signal what we care the most about. We see something that shouldn't be, and we do something about it. Maybe, just maybe, who you are is a person created to solve a certain problem.

Your job may put food on your table, but it may not be the problem you were called to solve. What moves you to action? What lights your fire? What do you feel God has made you for? Do you come alive when you're serving the homeless in your community? Or leading on your church's worship team? Do you serve at a home for battered women and feel, *This is it!* Or maybe you're fostering children to show them the love of Christ, or working in the youth ministry at church to develop the lives of teenagers. For you, it might be tutoring kids after school to help them get their education back on track. What makes you come alive whenever you have the opportunity to solve a particular problem?

Joseph felt moved to do something about the conditions he saw in each place — whether it was running a household, bringing order to a prison, or feeding a hungry country. The needs he saw moved him to action. As a matter of fact, the reason he was made a leader was because *he was already leading.* He was noticed doing things a leader does.

One of the ways we can find our purpose in life is to recognize what moves us to action. What are we already doing? If you have a dream but are not acting on that dream, then it's just a daydream.

Every summer in June, our church puts on the Greatest Show on Earth, an event geared toward kids who won't get to take a summer vacation. We have a free petting zoo, snow cones, hot dogs, carnival rides, and superheroes walking around, taking photos with the kids. It's not enough to care about people. As followers of Jesus, we must take action to have a positive impact on people's lives, meeting their physical, emotional, and spiritual needs.

Joseph's dream did not come to fruition until he was thirty years old, thirteen years after he saw his dreams. But during that time, he didn't just sit around waiting; he was active. My call to preach began with a wild vision of me standing in a pulpit before thousands of people, not just the grass and a few hedges in our yard. It took a few years to come to fruition, but God continued to reinforce my divine purpose in numerous ways — other people, opportunities, and results were blessed by his favor.

When Joseph was seventeen, he was trying to discover who he was. He had to push through the curveballs life threw at him. But his trials and obstacles didn't slow him down. In fact, when he was reunited with his brothers decades later, Joseph said, "You intended to harm me, *but God* intended it for good to accomplish what is now being done, the saving of many lives" (Gen. 50:20). When we're living out the dream God has given us, even our problems can have purpose.

Bringing God Glory

Our identity should always be wrapped up in God's purpose: advancing his kingdom, sharing the gospel, and serving others. This is true no matter what your dream is. We're all parts — different parts — of the same body, helping and complementing one another.

No matter what you do — whether you're a CEO, a

minister, a custodian, a mom — it's about changed lives. Your identity is to bring God glory no matter what you do. "And whatever you do or say, do it as a representative of the Lord Jesus, giving thanks through him to God the Father" (Col. 3:17 NLT).

So what is it you're chasing now? How do you define yourself? If you're not experiencing the level of contentment that comes from doing what God created you to do, then I encourage you to return to your dreams and rekindle the sparks of greatness he ignited in you. If you know what you love doing, what you're good at, what you are passionate about, then you know your God-given purpose.

Too often, we chase after what the world calls success to give our lives meaning, but God is the only One who can give us the passionate purpose that will ultimately satisfy us. We fall short of our full potential to lead a joyful and kingdom-impacting life not because we're careless dreamers, but because we're careful realists settling for too little. If you want more satisfaction, more meaning, more joy in your life, then live out of who your Creator made you to be. If you want to experience real fulfillment, then passionately pursue your God-given purpose!

5

We Lose Our Way...
But God Guides Us

*Trust in the LORD with all your heart and lean not on
your own understanding; in all your ways submit to him,
and he will make your paths straight.*

PROVERBS 3:5–6

Not so long ago my wife had a "but God" encounter that
reminded both of us that even though we may know our
divine purpose, we can still lose our way. We can get
distracted, disconnected, and disappointed with our life
circumstances and lose our focus on what matters most
—our relationship with God. That's what happened to
Tiffany.

I was driving home, looking forward to a good hot meal
and some downtime with my family. With the autumn

days getting shorter, the darkness of an Oklahoma night enveloped me as I reflected on the day's conversations, meetings, and plans. My day had been a challenge by noon, and I wanted nothing more than to leave it all behind and just relax around the table with Tiffany and our kids. My wife might never have her own show on the Food Network, but the girl can definitely put together a dinner that our family thoroughly enjoys.

Pulling into our driveway, I smiled to myself, thinking about the way Tiffany and the kids always made me glad I was home. I turned the key to "off" in the ignition and opened the garage door to the house, greeted immediately by — nothing. No scurrying kids' footsteps, no scent of delectable foods wafting from the kitchen. The house was quiet, dark. I dropped my bag on the bench in the hallway and began walking through the house.

"Tiffany?" I called.

Nothing.

Walking into the living room, I was greeted only by the Disney Channel. The TV lights flickered vividly against the walls in the dark room. This was definitely not the norm. My heart beat faster as I sensed something was wrong. "Tiffany?" I called again, remembering that she had never answered my text to tell her I was on my way home.

"Daddy, she's right there," my youngest said, popping around the corner and pointing at the couch.

Sure enough, Tiffany was lying on the couch with her eyes closed, a hand on her forehead. I sighed with relief before feeling a different worry creep back up on me. She slowly turned her head to look at me.

"Honey," she whispered, "I'm so sorry. You know I wouldn't be doing this if I didn't have to … I'm just feeling awful. There's no way I'm gonna be able to cook dinner or take care of anyone tonight. I only stayed out here because I knew I needed to be close to the kids."

I nodded and sat next to her. We quickly talked through her symptoms: dizziness, lightheadedness, exhaustion. After I helped Tiffany move to our bedroom where it was dark and quiet, I took the kids to the kitchen and did what any resourceful dad would do — ordered pizza (and breadsticks, as I recall). But more than hunger gnawed in my stomach as we waited for dinner.

Something was very wrong with my wife.

Out of It

Before I continue, I should tell you a little bit about Tiffany. She is the very definition of trooper, the type who "pushes through" an illness and barely lets it slow her down. There's nothing high maintenance about her. Usually, I'm the one nagging her to rest and take better care of herself. Once Tiffany had a terrible migraine, the kind that renders others helpless, and yet she endured her extreme discomfort to visit first-time guests at church with me. She battled colds and the flu, pushing through to take care of the kids and keep everyone on their normal routine.

As I thought about it that night, I had noticed the last few weeks that something was a little off with Tiff. Happy and contented by nature, she had seemed a bit disconnected and "out of it." Whenever I brought it up, though, she'd said, "As soon as we get past next Sunday and those events coming up, then I can slow down. I'll be okay." So, reluctantly, I had let it go, but then I'd notice the following week that she still seemed to be lagging behind her usual self.

She slept through that night and felt better the next day, well enough to go on our usual date night. On the way home, I asked her how she was doing. She started off a little general, the usual "I'm okay." But after the last few weeks, especially the previous night, I wasn't accepting "I'm okay" anymore.

I continued to ask questions, and we reached a breakthrough in our conversation. "I don't really know what's going on with me. I'm not excited about anything. I'm not feeling joy for life. I'm not ... anything. I'm just here. I've never felt like this before, Herbert, and I really don't know what's going on." Her brown eyes looked at me straight on, and it was obvious she was struggling.

The revelation that she hadn't been herself for a while made me a little nervous. Strike that. A lot nervous. What were we dealing with here? Depression? Some physical illness? Both? Her need for a "but God" encounter created a need for one of my own! I wanted God's reassurance that my beautiful wife would find out what was going on and how to overcome it. She was clearly in a funk. I had no idea what it was.

Spinning the Plates

Ultimately, we realized that Tiffany needed to see a doctor to get to the bottom of her physical symptoms.

Secretly, I continued to fear that with all the headaches and dizziness, there could be something seriously wrong. I both welcomed and dreaded the doctor appointments. I felt caught in between what I wanted to happen — my wife to return to normal — and what the doctor might find. Once again, I found myself crying out to God for his help, his reassurance, his peace.

Tiffany's doctor did a full range of blood tests and found that she was low in Vitamin D, something that can affect mood. When her doctor told her that this could be stress-related, Tiffany quickly said, "I'm not that stressed. I'm good." I think at the time she believed what she was saying.

She was referred to an ear, nose, and throat specialist to shed some light on her ongoing dizziness. This doctor diagnosed her with Meniere's disease, an inner ear disorder that affects balance and hearing. It can be brought on by a number of things, one of them being — you guessed it — stress.

Please understand that Tiffany truly did not consider stress a factor in her life. She had always kept a lot of plates spinning at the same time and handled them all gracefully. In hindsight, though, we began to realize the cumulative effects of her various roles and responsibilities. With each child we had, and with each year that People's Church grew, she took on a few additional duties. It's easy not to notice the gradual addition of stress when you continue to take on just "one more thing," but eventually it piled up on her.

While we were relieved that the problem was as simple as stress, we both knew that "fixing" someone's stress level is not a simple task. So we decided to sit down together to examine a little more closely the things in her life and her schedule.

The idea that stress was not only affecting her but was also creating problems for those she loved was an eye opener for Tiffany. This was something she had tried to avoid. She told me that as things got busier, she'd keep from dropping the ball on the kids or on me by staying up later or getting up earlier to fit everything into her day. She, in effect, ended up dropping the ball on herself.

After much prayer and processing, Tiffany realized she needed to take this problem seriously. She needed to cut down on the number of things she was doing. Without realizing it, Tiff had taken on too much. She and I were both reminded that even though we know our divine purpose, we can still lose our way.

Living with the End in Mind

My lovely wife was at a crossroads. How could she ever balance the roles of mom, wife, leader of different ministries, friend ... and not take on too much? Clearly, those first two roles alone encompass unlimited responsibilities. It would be easy for her to slip back into thinking, *Sure, I can handle "one more thing."* But Tiffany's "but God" moment helped her to understand that she needed to determine which things were most important. She needed to identify where she was headed in life, what her priorities should be. Ultimately, Tiffany realized that if she was going to get her stress level under control, she had to use a different road map. She needed a new route that kept her focused on her destination.

As many of us have found out, a GPS system is only as good as its source map. If the map is outdated or inaccurate, we may end up getting directions to Edmonton, Calgary, in Canada instead of Edmond, Oklahoma, in the good old USA. Or we may know our destination, but sometimes we end up losing our way. We know where we're headed, but life gets in the way, and we shift into default mode — staying busy, going with the flow. We let the expectations of others determine our route instead of seeking the guidance of the One who made us.

Living On Purpose

If you are not living your life focused on your destination, then you wander through life, going where life takes you instead of living life FOR a purpose and ON purpose. You lose sight of the big picture. You wake up one day and realize you don't like your life. You've drifted with the current and you now struggle to find the solid ground that was once in sight.

If that's you — if you are unhappy with a certain aspect of your life or maybe even your life in general, you need to ask yourself, "Does my daily routine align with my commitment to follow Jesus and his priorities for my life?"

When we get pulled in so many directions, we face the same choice confronted by Jesus' friends Mary and Martha. Wanting to be the perfect hostess, Martha tried to keep the plates spinning as she cooked the meal, set the table, and made all the necessary preparations. Her sister,

Mary, stayed close to their guest, listening and talking and soaking up the wisdom of the Messiah. When Martha complained about her "lazy" sister to Jesus, he said, "Martha, Martha ... you are worried and upset about many things, but few things are needed — or indeed only one. Mary has chosen what is better, and it will not be taken away from her" (Luke 10:41 – 42).

Before you're tempted to judge Martha, think about your own life and all the activities, responsibilities, and obligations that keep you busy. Are they all necessary? Despite our best intentions, sometimes we lose sight of God and his priorities for our life. We subtly shift our priorities from what he calls us to do and end up doing what others want us to do or what we *think* God wants us to do. Both Martha and Mary obviously cherished their friendship with Jesus, but Martha lost sight of what was most important — spending time with Jesus — and became distracted by being a good hostess, preparing a delicious meal, being prepared and organized.

We've all been here. Jesus doesn't have to come to our house for dinner for us to experience this dilemma. We become so focused on the urgent busyness of life — what we perceive we must do — that we miss what God wants from us. When we allow other people, additional responsibilities, and "kingdom work" to define our Christian faith, then we've set ourselves up to fail. When we follow these other push-pull forces and try to please everyone, our attention, energy, and time get fragmented into little pieces that slowly erode our soul's peace.

So how do you stay focused on what matters most? Obviously, the Bible gives us great wisdom on how to live our lives. Throughout it we are told to make it a priority to love God, treat other people out of that love, walk in a way that honors God, and tell people about God (see Matt. 22:37 – 39). These are expectations that he has of all of us. Before we become pulled into an overload of good activities, it's essential for us to regularly remind ourselves of God's priorities for us and to put them into our spiritual GPS so that we are following the right map.

Back to the Future

As you assess whether your current lifestyle aligns with God's priorities, consider where you will wind up if you keep living the way you're living now. Will you become the person God has called you to be by continuing to do what you're doing? If not, then consider where you want to be as you look ahead. What do you *want* your life to look like a year from now? Five years? Ten? *Twenty?* When you think about your life now, is there something specific that's out of sync with your faith and who God wants you to be? Perhaps you have an estranged relationship with a relative. Maybe you are in a dating relationship that is not going the way you wish it would. Or maybe you're not happy with the way your career is going. Possibly you have financial issues you'd like to improve — paying off debt or saving for a home. Perhaps you want to improve your family life. Maybe you're unhappy, knowing you're not doing what you were created to do.

While there's no magic formula for how to experience a "but God" realignment, I've found a clue in one of my favorite verses from the Psalms. "Take delight in the

LORD, and he will give you the desires of your heart" (Ps. 37:4). It's easy to read this verse and see only the second part of it. Some people use the second half of that verse to encourage others, saying things like, "God's gonna give you the desires of your heart! Just you wait and see!" But the verse has two parts. First, you must delight yourself in the Lord. What does that mean, exactly?

Please understand that the word *delight* is not just a synonym for *happy*. I believe it refers to joy. If you "take delight" in the Lord, this means you take "great pleasure" in the Lord. You enjoy spending time getting closer to God through the Word and in prayer, and these things don't feel like tasks to you. You take pleasure in worshiping God, serving others, and using your resources for God's kingdom. When knowing and loving God is your greatest delight, the desires of your heart will line up with his Word and his purpose for you.

So let me ask you some of those questions again. What do you want your life to look like? Where do you want to be in one, five, ten, twenty years from now? Seek God with all your heart and ask him to line up your desires with his. What do you want for your career, relationships, and your finances? Do they line up with God's desires for you, the ones he's revealed to you through prayer, Scripture, and other believers? Are your desires consistent with his Word?

If you can see total alignment, then full speed ahead. Take the purpose God has revealed to you and let it be the engine that drives your daily routines and responsibilities. Think about who God wants you to be and where he wants to take you, then use that as your GPS coordinates. That's where you're going, so begin with the end in mind.

When you know where you want to end up, you remove the guesswork on how to get there. This is not a matter of "keeping options open." If you don't have a clear target, anything is acceptable. If you say yes to everything, even things that might be good in the short term could cause you to burn out.

That's what happened to Tiffany. She was focusing on too many tasks. She was not putting first things first. Most of us have done the same thing at one time or another. These tasks may be wonderful endeavors that further God's kingdom — things like serving, teaching, and leading — but are not the unique ones he calls us to do. Like Martha cooking and preparing for Jesus' visit, we're doing good things for the right reasons, but have lost sight of our primary calling.

If we don't learn to say no to things that don't align with God's calling for our life, then we'll get overloaded and overwhelmed. Yes, this may mean disappointing some people along the way. It's going to take guts. I encourage you to think through your priorities and compare them to how you spend your time, your energy, and your resources.

Set a New Course

After the doctor's diagnosis, Tiffany and I discussed all that she was doing.

One of the reasons she took on so much may have been her desire to be the perfect pastor's wife and mother, a superwoman who never says no and handles every task with a smile. Another may have been her assumption that she should say yes to every faith-related request that came her way.

The misalignment between Tiffany's top priorities and her schedule suddenly seemed clear. But it took a health crisis to show us just how far she had drifted from her most precious priorities — her relationship with Christ, her marriage, and her kids. Even though she was praying, reading her Bible, and pursuing God, she allowed the current of too many activities to propel her away from her true calling.

This conversation was a clear "but God" turning point for Tiffany, for me, and for our family. Thinking about who God had made her to be, where she wanted to be in the near and distant future, and what God had revealed to her as her purpose helped her to reestablish her life's GPS coordinates. She knew that God had called her to be a wife and mother first. While she also has the gifts of leading, teaching, and writing, she realized she doesn't have to exercise them all at every opportunity. Since she knew that our marriage and parenting are core to her God-given priorities, some key questions helped her to understand how to live them out each day. What kind of marriage did she want? What does this look like day to day? What kind of mom does she want to be for our children? What daily habits and consistent practices contribute to being this kind of woman? Through delighting ourselves in the Lord, we knew the answers to most of these questions, so it just became a matter of figuring out how to live them day by day.

This is the tricky part. The address we put into our life's GPS each day is crucial to our success. It's easy to have good intentions and yet not follow through. It can be daunting to see the distance between where we are and where God wants us to be. But if our daily routes don't line up with our destination, then we'll never get there.

Usually, we are better able to spot when other people's actions and priorities are out of alignment than we are when it comes to seeing how our own actions and priorities are skewed. Know any people who thought they were headed in a certain direction toward a goal but never got there? Everyone around them could see that they were headed the wrong way, but they couldn't. "The prudent see danger and take refuge, but the simple keep going and pay the penalty" (Prov. 27:12).

We've all heard excuses like these and perhaps even said them ourselves:

- "But it's love!"
- "I just need some time to figure out who I am."
- "But I won't get addicted."
- "Sure, I can just add one more thing to my plate."
- "But I deserve a night with the boys. I can't miss my softball league."

Chances are good that these people haven't delighted themselves in the Lord and figured out their ultimate GPS address. If they had, it would be more obvious to them when they were making a bad decision. As one of my favorite pastors, Andy Stanley, says, "Everything is headed in a direction. The outcome is predictable." Will these excuses and behaviors get these people to where they really want to go?

Sometimes we have to say no to some good opportunities in order to say yes to our God-given priorities. Consider each daily choice that comes your way with the end in mind. What if a "really great job" with more pay opens up that will require lots of hours away from your family? Yes, the pay increase will provide a lot of material possessions for you and your family, but you will be absent from your family for weeks at a time. Is missing out on time with your family worth that extra amount of money? Here's another example. If you want your kids to know and love God, is it most effective for you to miss church all summer so they can play ball? Sports are great, but they can't compare with the eternal significance of knowing God. Or if you want to pay off your debts, should you open a new store credit card for 20 percent off your purchase? You get the idea.

I know these are hard questions. The "right" answers are not easy. Just remember your destination, your end goal. View your choices and opportunities through that lens. Which decision will get you closer to your goal? Which decision will take you further away?

Following Directions

Tiffany and I answered those questions together, and Tiffany's "but God" moment occurred when she realized that her excess stress resulted from saying yes to too many things that weren't aligned·with her goals. That "but God" encounter caused her to input her spiritual

GPS destination — raising four God-loving kids, maintaining a healthy and happy marriage, and doing a knockout job at the ministries she oversees at People's Church. So instead of looking at opportunities to see if she can fit them into her schedule, she now makes decisions with her spiritual destination in mind.

Before Tiff's "but God" moment, it had seemed like a good idea for her to fill up her social calendar and meet with as many women in the area as possible. In addition, she was volunteering many hours each week to assist a new ministry that was dear to her heart. And she was to speak at a women's conference in Florida that she expected would be fun and beneficial.

Problem was, she already had another trip planned for the month of the women's conference. Not only would she had have the stress of preparing another speech, she would have the added burden of prepping to leave four kids behind and communicate their schedules and needs to another person who would be with them while she was gone. Two trips in one month might seem like the correct choice for becoming an awesome conference speaker. But that was not her goal.

Tiffany reprogrammed her priorities. She is now able to say no to good opportunities that are not aligned with her God-given priorities. As good as these things would be, they would take her off course from where she truly wants to be.

It helps to have people around you who know your goals. If you are trying to save up for a car so you won't have a car loan, don't go shopping with the person who says, "Oh, you deserve that new purse/iPad/[insert desired item here]." Instead, surround yourself with people who will help you make a U-turn when necessary. "If either of them falls down, one can help the other up. But pity anyone who falls and has no one to help them up" (Eccl. 4:10).

Tiffany has a few good friends who know what she went through. They often check in with her to make sure she's not saying yes to too many things. I remind her to say no to some things that are good so that she can say yes to better things. God allowed Tiffany to see that she had veered off course. She had added too many new destinations to her route, creating anxiety, stress, and health problems.

If you look at your opportunities and choices through the lens of your final goal, you too will know how to stay on course. Your journey is going to take some time, so check your progress from time to time. Make sure that little dot on the map is still on the path. Even with great GPS instructions, it's possible to accidentally veer off course. It's easy to start listening to the voices of people and the sounds of good opportunities and to tune out the voice of the Holy Spirit. When this happens, you have to figure out how to get back on course. You need to stop, find out where you went wrong, and allow the gentle voice of the Spirit to redirect your steps toward God's priorities for your life.

So, where are you going? Remember that God has certain expectations for you. Seek him first. What desires is he putting in your heart? What do you want to change? Your answers will reveal what your destination needs to be. Plug it into your GPS and make the right choices to get there. We're told, " 'No eye has seen, no ear has heard, and no mind has imagined what God has prepared for those who love him.' *But ... God* has revealed them to us by his Spirit" (1 Cor. 2:9 – 10, emphasis mine). I know this is talking about what God has planned for us in eternity, but God also comes to us during our lives here on earth.

If you seek God and find joy in him, his Spirit will speak to you and reveal things to you. If you have a "but God" course correction, remember it has to be lived out each and every day. Check your divine coordinates each day and stay focused on your God-given priorities. Then you won't have to worry about getting lost. No matter where you are, with God guiding you, you're on your way!

6

We Seek Relationships...
But God Gives Us
Divine Connections

Walk with the wise and become wise,
for a companion of fools suffers harm.

When I first became a Christian, I was "all in." I didn't want to continue living the way I was living. Even as a teenager, I knew I needed to change my surroundings, including people. The guys I had been hanging out with didn't understand the major changes I was making. They knew only that I didn't want to chase girls with them like I used to.

It wasn't that I avoided these people or was mean to them in any way. We still talked — some of them were on the football team with me — but I no longer wanted to hang out and spend significant, influential time with them. I knew I wasn't strong enough to stand firm in my new faith if I continued letting others influence me to do things I knew God didn't want me to do.

So I altered those relationships and tried to get clarity on God's plan for my life. I understood that part of that plan was to live a lifestyle that would honor Jesus, and that I couldn't honor him by continuing in my old habits and hanging out with my running buddies.

It was lonely at times. I didn't want to be "that guy, the Jesus freak" or have others think that I felt like I was better than they were. I didn't; I simply knew how weak I was. And I seemed to be reminded frequently of my weakness, creating opportunities for more "but God" experiences in my life. After crying out to God, I soon realized that there were other people like me who were committed to following Jesus with the same passion and intensity. These people had dedicated their lives to loving God and following Christ just as I had done. They were my brothers and sisters in the faith, men and women serving the Lord and forming the body of Christ, the church.

In my early years as a new Christian, I appreciated the connection to others just as passionate about their faith as I was about mine. In my local church, and then once I started college, I found teachers, role models, mentors, and special friends who encouraged me, challenged me, and inspired me. My relationships with the people in this circle differed from my earlier friendships. We shared the most important thing of all. We wanted God's best for one another. We understood the difficulties of living out our faith in a culture that doesn't always like what we have to say. These people weren't perfect, and my relationships with them were not without conflicts. However, ultimately we knew we were part of something bigger, a spiritual family of God's children.

Everyone has relationships, but God wants us to experience the struggles, sacrifices, and satisfaction that come from living in a committed community. Our Creator knows that we were designed to be social beings, to be in authentic relationships with one another. God himself is comprised of the Trinity of Father, Son, and Holy Spirit. He created us in his own image, and since the moment Adam and Eve appeared on the earth, God has pursued his children to have an intimate relationship with him. He wants us connected to him but also connected and committed to one another.

I'm convinced God sometimes brings special people — divine connections — into our lives to help us grow stronger and wiser, to be more authentic, and to accomplish amazing feats that we couldn't accomplish on our own. I call these special friendships "but God" relationships because God often uses these people to transform our lives and at times even to alter the course of our lives. These people serve as catalysts, facilitators, encouragers, and providers in fulfilling our God-given purpose and priorities.

Divine connections are those pivotal, destiny-altering friendships that God brings into our lives from time to time. These people seem to show up in our lives at just the right moment — not necessarily when we want them to — and they remind us that we're not alone. They become fellow travelers on our faith journey for a while — sometimes just for a short season, other times for years and years. This has certainly been my experience with a handful of special "but God" relationships over the course of my life. As I share some of them with you, I'm reminded of how God has used these individuals to deeply impact my life and ministry.

Travelers in the Same Direction

We all crave a connection that runs deeper than just a surface relationship, someone who seems to "get us" and appreciates how unique we are, a friend who enjoys our sense of humor, who can see into the heart of our struggles, and who's there for us when we are struggling. These people do more than just become our friends. They push us and spur us on to see our God-given dreams and priorities fulfilled. These individuals seem like members of our tribe, travelers committed to the same direction and destination in their journey toward God and his kingdom.

I found this kind of deep and special connection with Tiffany, and that led to my asking her to become my wife. The kind of relationship we have as husband and wife is a huge gift. She is my best and closest friend. Having her as my wife, my partner throughout all of life's ups and downs, remains the most wonderful, impactful "but God" relationship I've ever experienced.

However, a spouse isn't the only person who can give us this kind of life-giving relationship. Whether we are married, single, or divorced, we all need "but God" friendships to help us move forward in life and to help us see our God-given dreams come to pass. These people reveal, reinforce, and remind us of our unique gifts and talents and how we can use them to make a difference in the world for God's kingdom.

And church isn't the only place to find these kinds of "but God" connections. In fact, I never expected to find rich fellowship and a powerful connection with a fellow believer in a van full of white Christian rock musicians. But that's exactly where I found Terry Kelley. I had just finished preaching at a church camp where Terry was the guest worship leader. Camps are busy prospects, and we hadn't spent a lot of time talking until that last night as we were wrapping things up. But it didn't take long to realize that we were having a significant conversation despite having met only a few days before. I'm not even sure I could tell you what we talked about; I just knew that conversation was the beginning of more to come.

My connection with Terry in this conversation struck me as a "but God" moment, an awareness that God had brought us together to encourage, support, and strengthen one another. I knew without a doubt that we could help each other make a greater impact for God's kingdom. Terry was an immediate "but God" friend for me and my ministry despite our many differences.

Never in a million years would I have expected to be friends with a creative "artsy" type. I am a concrete person, thinking in black and white all the time. Terry is an artist. But somehow we understood each other. We both had more passion than experience at that time and were working hard trying to establish ourselves on the road. We were both trying to do something significant for God, and there was a sense that we'd run into each other again somewhere.

And we did.

An Unlikely Friendship

Terry and I ended up at quite a few of the same events, and even though we were responsible for two different parts of the service, we were working together. We would work together on stage, developing a flow, then after the service we'd hang with the pastor or person who had invited us to the event.

When we talked to these older, wiser Christian leaders, Terry and I were earnest, reflective, dedicated young disciples of Christ. But then when we'd head back to our hotel, we'd act like a couple of crazy guys. We'd play video games (don't get me started on how I dominate at Madden Football!), hang out with the rest of the band, and just let our hair down a bit after those conferences. Okay, I was sporting a short haircut that barbers call a "fade," so I didn't literally let my hair down, but you know what I mean. It was such an unlikely friendship, yet it worked beyond what I could have imagined.

Because we both lived in Springfield, Missouri, at the time and traveled from there, it made sense for us to share an office, and for a year we even shared a secretary. This worked well as both of our ministries were gaining steam. Terry and I would get back from our respective bookings at the beginning of the week, report in to our secretary, then swap stories about our latest adventures.

We'd go to a meeting hall outside our tiny office space

or we'd end up in a Chinese or Mexican restaurant — two types of restaurants suddenly everywhere in Springfield — and just talk. He and I discussed theology and shared our latest insight about God's Word. We dreamed about the future together and where God might lead each of us. It was an enormous blessing to be able to have a friend who could share so many aspects of my life.

Here was a person who was trying to do the same thing I was — follow Christ and share God's love with others — but with music. We were not in any way in competition, yet we were able to understand each other's worlds. They were the same world. We were able to have vulnerability in the friendship and to share our struggles and disappointments, our hopes and dreams and goals without fear because we were in the same place. We had the same things to lose or to gain. The more I got to know Terry, the more I realized his friendship was a gift from God. We could help each other, encourage each other, and just laugh and hang out. It was awesome.

Because Terry and I both traveled and did a lot of youth events, we were able to see God open doors for each of us that would not have opened without our connection. We often received queries from the coordinators of youth camps and youth conferences. I remember one time in particular when Terry got a call with an invitation to lead worship at a large youth convention. As he talked with the coordinator, he learned that they did not yet have a keynote speaker, so he recommended me. His recommendation became a "but God" experience as I ended up accepting the invitation to speak at that conference, which then led to many other ministry opportunities.

Terry continued to recommend me for speaking engagements and ministry events, all of which provided income for me and my family and eventually generated the financial backing to start People's Church.

Eventually, Terry and I both moved on into different ministries. Terry is now the worship pastor at a thriving church. We can go months without talking, but if I get on the phone and call him, we pick up right where we left off. And believe me, we still act stupid. The depth of friendship we had then and the fact that we both have continued to serve the Lord allow us to not miss a beat.

Above Average

The people we hang out with have a huge effect on what path we take. Motivational speaker Jim Rohn popularized the idea that we are the composite of the five people we are around the most. This notion reflects the age-old law of averages — we end up being the average of the people we hang around with the most. If we surround ourselves with people who don't challenge us — or worse, become a negative influence in our lives — then we're not going to grow the way we do when we encounter "but God" connections.

The Bible, particularly Proverbs, is heavily laden with advice about the people we run with. The number of verses on this topic underscore the incredible importance of this principle. Our friends will either make us better or they will make us worse. If we are trying to live intentionally and achieve goals that are aligned with God's dreams for us, we need to make sure that the people we hang out with are not putting up roadblocks, but instead are help-ing us to grow and achieve those goals.

So who are the people you are closest to in life?

Chances are those who know you best are fam-ily members, maybe a close friend or two, maybe even someone you work with, maybe someone you respect and admire. Are these people life-giving? Are they encourag-ing and positive? If so, the chances are good that you will be too. The opposite is true as well. If the people you are spending time with are cynical or bitter or negative, it's likely that these attitudes will rub off on you and affect your destiny.

Are the people you spend time with encouraging you in your God-given priorities and hopes? Do they nudge you toward the things God wants for you? Or do they do the opposite? I'm not talking about someone having a bad day or a bad patch in life. We've all heard of the Debbie Downer or the Stick in the Mud. You can assess if you're spending your time around the right people based on their effect on you. Are you spending a lot of time with someone who is gossiping and negative and hate-ful? Do you leave your time with that person drained and exhausted?

If you're around a Debbie Downer all the time, it will affect your outlook on the world around you. The apos-tle Paul warns us: "Do not be misled: 'Bad company cor-rupts good character'" (1 Cor. 15:33). Bad company rubs off on you just like good company does. Negativity and pessimism will rub off. You will find yourself pulled into negative thinking.

Or maybe you will find yourself pulled into the same

behavior, and instead of enjoying the life God has given you, you start complaining, griping, and whining about life. The Bible tells us if we walk with the wise, we will become wise, but a friend of the foolish will suffer harm (Prov. 13:20). Hanging around with the "foolish" will cause a person to become foolish because bad company corrupts good character.

Your relationships should be directing you to your divine destination. When you have encountered a "but God" transformation by committing your life to Christ, when you have discovered your God-inspired priorities and who he wants you to be, it's critical that the people with whom you spend the most time will push you toward those priorities. Keep in mind that all relationships take work. Even when God brings divine connections into our lives, we have to work on communication, conflict resolution, and how best to encourage one another. All of these actions take effort, but the payoff is immeasurable.

"Not God" Relationships

You may have good character, good intentions, good motives, and good dreams, but if you are consistently around the wrong people, they will put water on your fire. They will corrupt your good character, your good intentions and motives and dreams. If you are spending time with someone who consistently brings you down or encourages you to make poor decisions, it's time to reconsider why you are continuing to invest so much time and energy in a relationship that is pulling you away from God's plan for your life.

We have to watch who we hang around. Sometimes we need to end or significantly change a relationship because it is negative, and we need to make room in our life for people who have a positive impact on us. While this may sound basic and obvious, in actuality it can be painful and challenging to recognize when someone — maybe someone who used to encourage you — is dragging you down with negativity, pessimism, and destructive (not constructive) criticism. I remember when People's Church was running about 400 people. I had a friend who was also a pastor, and when we started People's Church, he and I were good friends. We talked on the phone frequently, and he would give me great advice. However, I began to notice that as the size of People's Church approached the size of his church, his advice began to change.

As we continued to talk, the vibe felt different. His tone became more critical and comparative, more defensive and authoritarian. He could not "rejoice with those who rejoice" (Rom. 12:15). There was no happiness for the God-successes at People's Church. I would end the call and feel awful. The relationship had become toxic. I ultimately had to disconnect from that friend because he was trying to take me in a direction I knew the Lord didn't want me to go. A hard decision, but the right one.

Seasonal Relationships

Sometimes a relationship may not be toxic to you or negative in any way, but you move on because the relationship was just for a certain time in your life, a season. We only have so much time and energy to invest in relationships. My relationship with my buddy Terry is different than it used to be. He and I used to talk almost every day. It was a destiny-fulfilling relationship. God was clearly and directly using us in each other's lives to become the men he wants us to be. But given the realities of our families and ministries, we knew that our "but God" friendship would eventually change.

Now we are both married and between us have lots of kids — we took that verse about "multiplying and being fruitful" to heart! Our season of life changed, and so our investment in our relationship has changed. I love Terry, love talking to him, and I'm excited that God is doing incredible things in his life. But now we talk less often because we are in a different season. We both understand this.

If we're not willing to let our relationships change and grow and develop, then we may be blocking the blessings God has for us. Clinging to the past, trying to relive memorable moments, and constantly dwelling in the old "glory days" is not healthy for either person in a friendship. If you're both committed to God's best for one another, then you have to be willing to allow friends to come and go. When we encounter a "but God" connection with another person, we must also realize that friendship may change over time.

Seasonal friends can offer us godly wisdom and encourage us to grow closer to God. Sometimes they are people we meet while working on a project. When the project ends, so does the relationship. But as we look back, we can clearly identify the friendship as a "but God" connection that propelled us forward. Other seasonal friends include people whose paths we cross because of common life experiences. Sometimes these people are ahead of us in our life and faith journey and can serve as our mentor. Other times, we may be their encourager to guide through a struggle we've already faced.

Sometimes the Holy Spirit may prompt us to pursue a friendship with someone without us understanding the reason. Occasionally, we may be led to seek out other believers who can teach us, guide us, or counsel us in some way. These relationships may already be established through church or some other common interest, but often we have to ask for more if we want to experience the blessings of a "but God" type friendship.

Circle of Wisdom

If we're going to be effective at reaching our destiny and fulfilling our God-given purpose, we need to keep our eyes wide open for "but God" relationships. We need to be receptive to encountering those people who are ahead of us on life's journey and glean from their experience. We need mentors with spiritual maturity who can invest in our lives. As C. S. Lewis observed, "The next best thing to being wise oneself is to live in a circle of those who are."[2]

If you have doubts about entering a mentoring relationship, ask yourself why you wouldn't want the chance to learn from a person who has experienced where you're headed. For instance, if you have adolescent children, why wouldn't you want a relationship with someone who has made it through the teenage years with their kids? We validate the need for mentors in business relationships, but they can be just as important in our personal life.

Keep in mind that knowledge is not the same as wisdom. We can read books and take classes to get knowledge, but wisdom requires applying that knowledge. A lot of people can rattle off five ways to have a great marriage, but a person who is living out those five ways in real time — that person has wisdom. Mentors are those who not only pass on knowledge but they also give you wisdom on how to flesh out that information in day-to-day life. They're willing to show their vulnerability about their own mistakes in an effort to help you avoid the same kinds of missteps.

Sometimes God provides these key mentoring relationships in our lives even before we realize our need. I experienced this with my Uncle James and Aunt Janice, of whom I have many fond memories. They lived just over an hour away and would drive down with their two daughters, my cousins, just to hang out at our house. We would go fishing, horseback riding, play games, and tell family stories punctuated by a lot of laughter. My family went to visit them too. I can remember spending different spring breaks and holidays at their home.

During these times, while my cousins and other family members were outside or playing games, I'd hang behind just to hang out with my uncle. I remember sitting in his living room, listening to him tell me things that would later shape my life.

I loved his practical, helpful advice about life. No one had ever talked to me that way. He talked about buying cars and how I should always do it debt-free. He explained that I could buy ten used cars with cash before I could pay off a brand-new one. If I bought a $400 car and it broke down, no problem — buy a $600 car and pay cash for it. If that car broke down, no problem — buy a $1,000 car. He taught me that if I wanted to buy a new car, I should work my way there and not go into debt to do it. This was a huge "but God" moment for my financial future. Up to that point, no one had invested in my life regarding finances. God used these conversations to shape my financial trajectory.

My uncle taught me to spend less than I earned and to live within my means. He told me not to worry about keeping up with the Joneses because the Joneses are broke and just trying to look good on the outside. He said it in a kind, non-judgmental way, but I was picking up what he was throwing down. He talked about living life without debt as much as possible.

I would soak up this advice, trying to make sure I would remember all of it since the ideas were new to me. My uncle had no idea how profound, how powerful those conversations were to me. This relationship had immediate dividends in my life. I committed to living beneath my means. I set priorities and began saving for my future while most of my peers were spending money recklessly. I had the right person telling me the right things, and it led to one of the biggest "but God" moments of my life.

I'm not sure what kind of financial story I'd have if it weren't for the willingness of my Uncle James to give some time and advice to a teenager. I could've been in the backyard with the other teenagers, or I could've been at the table playing a card game with other family members, but I was drawn to this person who I knew was wise. His powerful words of wisdom have produced "but God" after "but God" after "but God" moments in my life.

Because of this "but God" relationship, Tiffany and I were completely out of debt — no student loans, no credit cards, no car payments — in our early twenties. Once we were debt-free, we bought our first home. With our mortgage as our only debt, we were able to save money like crazy so we could underwrite the launch of People's Church, which we still pastor today. The first year of People's Church, I didn't receive a salary. I traveled and preached and took speaking engagements to help fund the church and to provide for Tiffany and our family. The second year, I received a limited part-time salary so we could continue to hire staff and build the ministry. Yes, this "but God" connection with my Uncle James continues to have a ripple effect in my life, in my family's well-being, and on the impact of our church ministry.

Looking for Mentors

While God sometimes brings people into our lives without our asking, we often have to go looking for people, knocking on various relational doors to see which ones God opens. We must be proactive in seeking out individuals from whom we can learn, especially when we're looking for a teacher, a mentor, a practical guide or counselor.

When Tiffany and I moved to Oklahoma City to start People's Church, we started on that first Sunday, May 12, 2002, with 65 people. I knew the value of seeking out people who have done what I'm doing, so within six months, I called the local pastor at Life Church, Craig Groeschel, and asked to speak with him. We ended up meeting for lunch at a Bennigan's, and I asked him, "How do I reach more people far from God and get more people to come to People's Church? Like 200 people?" He answered, "YOU have to grow."

"Okay, great. How about 500?"

"YOU have to grow."

I wanted to ask about 1,000 people, but I was starting to get his point.

We met from time to time, and I hung on every word he said. I valued those meetings. I was willing to listen, learn, and apply what he was telling me. I think part of the reason he continued to meet with me was because I never talked about myself and tried to impress him. I came with pen and paper and a list of questions.

I've learned that people who have grown in wisdom can recognize people who know they need to grow in wisdom too — and boy did I ever need to grow! I didn't abuse the relationship by calling or texting Craig constantly, monopolizing his time. I just used the time we had wisely. I'd show up with my list of questions, ask them, then listen.

I don't know why Craig was willing to spend time with a new church planter in his own town, but I'm sure glad he did. I suspect it has something to do with his willingness to be used by God, to be a "but God" friend and mentor in my life. He never seemed to worry about whether I would be in competition with him. He was kingdom-minded from the beginning.

I still look up to Craig as a mentor. He is also a friend. It is invaluable to me to know that I have someone I can contact when (not if) I need his wisdom. I sought out and received the gift of his mentorship. Craig's relationship with me has produced many "but God" moments in my life and the life of People's Church.

One of the most vivid examples of how God used Craig's input comes from the early days when People's Church was growing rapidly and I was making logistical decisions. We had started the church in an AMC 24 movie multiplex and met in a smaller theater that seated 120 people. Before long, we quickly moved into a theater seating about 250 people. After a year we were growing at a rapid pace, and I wondered if we should move into a theater with capacity for about 600. It made sense and was doable, considering our venue.

I asked Craig for his thoughts about moving to a larger theater, totally unprepared for the "but God" moment about to occur. Craig told me not to move into the larger theater but to add a second service in our present location instead. He told me that our church would be healthier and grow faster with two services. He called it the "worship one and then serve one" concept. He said that scheduling a second service would create new opportunities for people to get plugged into the church because they would be able to use their gifts to serve others. Adding a second service meant we would need twice as many greeters, ushers, kids and youth volunteers, and so on. I heeded Craig's wisdom, and God poured out his blessings on our fledgling church as many more people became committed. In short, we grew like crazy!

Sometimes when we look back, we can appreciate our "but God" relationships more than we did at the time. In hindsight, we often see how we've developed, grown, and changed because of another person's investment in us. You might discover the kind of "but God" relationship you need in your life now by thinking through the key people who influenced you positively in the past.

Sam Jones was another important mentor to me earlier. Sam was a pastor in a nearby city. I learned that he and I belonged to the same gym. Now I'm no stalker, but I found out what time Sam was usually at the gym, and I'd show up then too if it worked in my schedule (of course it worked in my schedule!).

If he was working out arms one day, guess what? Me too! I'd just hope that Sam would say something to me, anything at all, and when he opened that door, I ran through it with a ton of questions. Often after his workout, he would end up talking to me for a half hour or more. He gave me great advice on kids, personal finances, marriage, health, church life, even how I could continue to do what I was doing and make it to old age with integrity and vitality. I overcame major hurdles as a young husband, father, and pastor because of this friendship.

Jim McNabb was another mentor with whom I developed a relationship that was pivotal to my destiny. Jim first had me preach at his church, The Bridge Church, at the youth service. While I was still in college, he had me back a couple of times to preach in the main service. After I graduated, married, and established my traveling ministry, he'd still invite me to preach.

One particular day, Jim and I were at lunch before I

was to leave town. I had just found out that I owed $500 for my quarterly taxes for self-employment. I was relatively new to being a self-employed, traveling preacher, and getting that tax bill was a shock to me. I had no idea that it was coming, and I also had no idea how I was going to pay it.

Tiffany and I were trying to keep up with our bills, but there wasn't an extra $500 sitting around somewhere that we could use to pay this one. In fact, Tiffany was in school full-time, and I was substitute teaching when I wasn't on the road. We were deeply in love and deeply broke. The money for this tax bill just wasn't there.

I always enjoyed my time with Jim and gained valuable insight and wisdom from him, but during this lunch, I was a little preoccupied. I just kept thinking, *How in the world am I going to pay this? I'll probably go to prison for tax evasion. It's a great preacher who can't pay his bills.*

Halfway through the meal, Jim leaned across the table, handed me a check, and said, "I want to bless your ministry." When I got to the car, I looked down, astonished to see that the check was written for exactly $500. What?! Jim had no prior knowledge of my situation. He was simply a mentor who had invested, and I was able to pay my tax bill.

Another time, Jim sent out letters to other pastors across the state, endorsing me as a speaker. Now that I'm a pastor too, I appreciate that gesture even more as I realize what a risk it was for him to tell these other pastors that they should bring a certain person in. His reputation was on the line in those letters too, not just mine. I booked several ministry engagements as a result of those letters and his belief in me. Jim was also one of the only pastors who gave money to People's Church back in its start-up days so that we could send a mailer to the community to invite them to our grand opening. Jim McNabb gave me wisdom, nurtured my traveling ministry, and helped us kick off our church plant. He was (and still is) encouraging to me.

When you have the right mentor, you have someone who believes in you and in what you're doing. A mentor will take you further, faster! I am where I am today because I'm standing on the shoulders of other men and women. I am not a self-made man. Nobody is. Even with the Bible as a guide, I needed (and still need) help.

If you long to be connected to people who can help you reach your God-given dreams and priorities, then ask God to send them your way. You don't have to be "Lone Ranger" Christian off doing your own thing. Maybe you grew up in a broken home and have not had many, or any, good examples of a strong marriage. Look for a couple who make their marriage work. If you're trying to start your own business and just need some answers, find a person who has already succeeded on this road. Maybe you don't have the parenting skills you need to get through the terrible twos or the teen years. Seek out another parent you admire and start up a conversation. See if it might be a good fit.

Pray and ask God to lead you to the right person, and then keep your eyes peeled for the individuals who cross your path. A "but God" relationship may already be under your nose, but you haven't recognized it yet!

Levels of Connection

The people we choose to do life with are not the same ones we "have" to do life with, such as family members or people we work with. The great thing about friends is that we get to choose them. Of course we want friends who are fun, but we also want people who are godly, who will understand us, support us, love us for who we are, and inspire us to be more of who God made us to be.

When you consider the various people in your life, consider who offers the opportunity for a "but God" relationship. There are different levels of how well we know a person, and that's usually linked to the size of investment we are making in that person. If you identify the various levels of relationship in your life, you will be better equipped to identify those people with whom you want to go deeper. You might also realize that God is moving someone from one level to another as you get better acquainted. Let's consider four different levels and how each is distinct from the others.

- **Level 4** connections are with people with whom you just chat about the weather, last night's baseball game, or some other current event. They may be casual acquaintances turned friends from the gym or your kid's school, or maybe your barista at the coffee shop. They may or may not turn into friends with whom you confide more about your life and faith.

- **Level 3** connections are those people with whom you share more personal experiences and information. These might include specific coworkers, neighbors you've known for a while, the parents of your kids' best friends. Once again, these not-so-deep friendships might progress into something more significant.

- **Level 2** connections are those people with whom you regularly share your struggles, your fears, your dreams, and your walk with the Lord. These may be siblings or extended family members, friends you've known for a long time, or people from your church or small group.

- **Level 1** connections are as real as it gets. A Level 1 friend is the person you can call in the middle of the night when you are distraught and can't sleep. This is the person who will put you first, themselves second, and try anything they can think of to help you.

When you get to this level, you're talking life! Marriage problems. Salaries. Career decisions. Parenting disasters. Personal struggles and temptations. These are the people you're calling at 11 p.m. when you're crying over the fight you had with your spouse or you're just burned out and hurt — this is gut-level friendship. This is bare-your-soul, you-love-me-for me-and-not-for-what-I've-done type of friendship. While you're also just having a blast together because all guards are down and you're just doing life together, these friendships can be the vehicle for some amazing "but God" moments. It's likely we experience this level of friendship only a few times in life.

Who's Got Your Back?

Everyone needs a Level 1 friend at some point, even a soon-to-be king. Jonathan was that kind of friend for David. These two men developed a friendship that allowed them to trust each other beyond any other person. The Bible says Jonathan "loved [David] as himself" (1 Sam. 18:1). This was a selfless, godly friendship.

Jonathan was the son of King Saul, the ruler of the Israelites, which meant Jonathan was supposed to be next in line for the throne. Over time David's successes in battle made him very popular with the people. King Saul, however, developed a deep jealousy of David, his successes, and the attention lavished upon him. He began to see David as a threat to his kingship and plotted to kill him. This is where David's need for a level 1 friend becomes imperative.

The plot to kill David goes on for chapters and chapters in the Bible. On more than one occasion, Jonathan saves David's life. He warns David at least once to flee. Another time he discovers Saul's plan and meets David to warn him yet again.

Jonathan is Saul's flesh and blood. However, he remains loyal to David and gives him his backing. Jonathan and David both devoted their lives and their service to the Lord. The Bible says Saul feared David because "the LORD was with David but had departed from Saul" (1 Sam. 18:12). Jonathan and David have their relationship with God as a commonality, and on top of that, they recognize traits they respect in each other.

Their friendship was close enough that Jonathan was the person David went to when he feared for his life: "What have I done? What is my crime? How have I wronged your father, that he is trying to kill me?" (1 Sam. 20:1).

This is that 11 p.m. phone call times ten! Jonathan put David first, himself second, and did whatever he could to help his friend. Talk about a "but God" relationship!

When I think of the Level 1 friends in my life, I think of Josh Brown. Josh does the executive operations at People's Church, and he has become not just an employee of the church where I'm the lead pastor but my friend and accountability partner. He's the guy I run everything past, anything that might be a little abnormal from my usual schedule and activities. He helps me think through choices and how I can set the best example as a pastor and follower of Christ.

For example, a couple years ago, I had a chance to meet several other senior pastors at a Dallas Cowboys football game, but it was going to be a quick trip, last minute, and I wouldn't be in Dallas for long. I also knew that the Monday night football game would end late, and then we'd get something to eat, and when we returned to the hotel we'd end up sitting in the lobby and talking for half the night. I wouldn't get to bed until two or three in the morning, and I'd be driving back to Oklahoma City at 8 a.m. I don't usually travel alone for accountability reasons, and so before I made my quick drive to Dallas and back in about twenty-four hours, I talked to Josh about it.

I made sure he thought it was reasonable for me to drive down alone to meet up with my pastor friends and then stay in a hotel alone before driving back. I had only one ticket to the game, so taking someone along would require that person to just wait around in the hotel room. After talking about it, Josh gave me his blessing.

Level 1 friendships are life-giving and key for us to get

to where God wants us to go. That's why it is important that your friends at this deep level are people who are committed to your faith and biblical values and dreams. If they aren't, then you are putting your dreams in the hands of the wrong people. Level 1 friends have to be the right friends, people God can use to strengthen and encourage you, or they may pull you away from your destiny.

Show me your friends and I'll show you your future.

The wrong relationships will pull you back, but the right relationships will push you forward. If you struggle with feeling frustrated as you try to accomplish your God-given dreams and goals by yourself, then ask God for some "but God" relationships. Ask him to surround you with people who will build you up, people you can trust, people you can encourage as well. Don't settle for average relationships when you can experience the divine connection of "but God" relationships!

7

We're Bound ...
But God Sets Us Free

It is for freedom that Christ has set us free.
Stand firm, then, and do not let yourselves
be burdened again by a yoke of slavery.

GALATIANS 5:1

I cracked open my bedroom door and peered into the dark hallway. The coast was clear. I nodded, and my partner in crime crept out of my bedroom, took the two quiet steps to the back door, and dashed into the night, where a friend waited to pick her up down the block.

This scenario happened frequently.

At some point during the time of my abuse, I started looking at dirty magazines (this is called pornography now, but back then we called them dirty magazines).

This was pre-Internet, so options were limited, but I was resourceful. By my sophomore year, I'd progressed from occasionally looking at dirty magazines to sneaking young women into my bedroom, which was not as difficult as you might think.

My dad had added a garage onto our home and was proud of the addition. Unwittingly, he had created the perfect escape route: my bedroom window now opened right into the garage. Plan B was the laundry room across from my bedroom, where the back door to our house was located. My bedroom was in the perfect location for a teenager trapped in sexual sin.

While I had installed a lock on my bedroom door for my own protection, it worked for other purposes as well. Sure, I had a curfew and rules to follow, but my parents never came near my bedroom. I don't know if they just trusted me because I made good grades and remained a disciplined athlete, or if they just thought teenagers wouldn't do that type of stuff. Regardless, I took advantage of my opportunities to be a major player in Wewoka.

I had an addiction to sex, a place that provided ample opportunity, and willing young women. What I didn't have was a way out of the darkness of my chronic behavior.

Power to Break Free

My sinful lifestyle started easily enough. During my sophomore year, I was asked to escort a senior to our prom —a *senior*. Talk about instant credibility! I pushed the boundaries of my parents' curfew that night and ended up getting busted, grounded, and shamed into promising I'd never do it again. So I laid low after the grounding was over, rebuilding my parents' trust and avoiding another belt-beating by my father. I didn't want to disappoint my mama again. I loved her too much to put her through the pain I'd seen in her eyes that night.

But then, after a little time passed, my parents relaxed, my desires kicked in, and I slipped out the door again. And again. This went on for two years.

While I thought I liked what I was doing, I discovered that my sexual escapades didn't leave me happy or make me feel fulfilled — not even close. Instinctively, I knew I didn't want my life filled up with empty sex. I wanted meaning and connection, intimacy, and what I was doing felt meaningless. In fact, each hookup made me feel less alive than I was before. One night as these thoughts ran through my head, I told the girl I was with, "I'm not gonna spend the rest of my life like *this*. I know this isn't the man I'm supposed to be."

Despite this realization, nothing changed. But a dissatisfaction, an awareness of wanting more, began to grow inside me. My feeling that night lit the fuse to an imminent "but God" encounter. As I look back on that feeling now, I'm convinced it was God trying to break into my life. He does that, you know. He'll do it again and again, speaking truth into our hearts. I heard him that night, I really did, but I didn't listen. I didn't want to hear what he had to say.

Fast-forward to a few months later. What I had half-realized that night could not be ignored. I needed help. Sex was not just a pleasurable act for me. It had become a way for me to escape, to numb the pain, to feel better. On my own, I could not break free of my addiction.

I was not able to break free until my senior year of high school when I experienced that locker room "but God" moment I told you about earlier. That night I realized that God had the power to change me—all of me! I knew I was forever set free. I was saved by faith in Christ, and the process of transformation had begun. I realized the way I had been living was not what I was created for. This truth was no longer just a thought that flittered through my head. It was *real*. I was too valuable to God to give myself away—and the girls I had been with were too. The Holy Spirit, God's Spirit, entered my life, and I broke free.

There's no rational explanation for it. I did not change because I had made a decision to change. My own will-power could not pull me away from the stronghold of my addiction. The change was supernatural. This doesn't mean I wouldn't be tempted in the future with these same behaviors. I would be. But my addiction no longer held the same power over me. I was changed.

Real Change Is Possible

This may be the most important chapter of the book. I want you to know, there is a supernatural God. We all want instructions on how to live a better life, how to improve where we're at, but sometimes we just need an *encounter* with Christ. The promise of the gospel is this: We bind ourselves up with false idols and pleasurable pursuits—sex, money, material possessions, or whatever

—but God sets us free. I realize that many people experience God but still battle addictions. Yet even when that's the case, when God enters our lives, he begins a process of supernatural transformation that will change us. God will strip away all the layers that prevent us from being the person he created us to be.

Although we can't break free from addictions and sinful habits by our own efforts, we can do our part to starve the appetite. What we feed grows, and what we starve dies. Before I came to Christ, I had been listening to all kinds of junk, filling my mind with sexual thoughts with music from 2 Live Crew, Heavy D, "Baby Got Back" ... (now, you KNOW what I'm talking about! Don't pretend you don't and put the book down!). I went from constantly listening to that stuff, stuff that encouraged and fed my addiction, to throwing all my cassette tapes away (if you don't know what cassette tapes are, they're an ancient mode of music that existed waaaay back in ... the '80s. They replaced vinyl records, and you could put one in a Walkman ... oh, never mind!). I threw away every recording I had of that type of music. Extreme? You bet it was! I didn't want to hear that stuff anymore. And I didn't want to leave myself open to any temptation they might ignite from my sexual addiction. I wanted to listen to Christian music, which is still my preference today. Sure, there are times when Tiffany and I break out some Marvin Gaye —you know, "let's get it on" music!—but God changed my ears as well as my heart.

Later I discovered my encounter with Christ was similar to the apostle Paul's conversion on the road to Damascus. In the Bible, in the book of Acts, we're told the story of a man named Saul who was committed to wiping out Christians. He persecuted those in the church, hunting down the followers of Jesus and taking them "as prisoners to Jerusalem to be punished" (Acts 22:5). He wanted them dead. Saul was feared.

But everything changed for Saul — and again, I mean *everything* — after his "but God" encounter with Jesus. He saw a vision of the resurrected Christ, and what followed was a complete 180-degree turn in his life. This bounty hunter's change was so dramatic, his life was so different, that after his conversion, his name was changed to Paul. His is one of the most dramatic conversions in the Bible, and today Paul is probably the most well-known apostle, someone who took the story of Jesus and the hope he brings (the gospel) from place to place until he finally was put to death for his faith.

God can instantly change a person's life. We're bound, but God sets us free. He did it with Paul, and he did it with me.

Get Desperate

Sometimes we just need to ask God, earnestly and sincerely with an open heart, to set us free. Jesus told us that if we ask, we will receive (Matt. 7:7). Obviously, this doesn't mean we can ask for vaults full of cash and expect God to be our magic genie. When our hearts are aligned with God's will and his truth in the Scriptures, our requests reflect his higher purposes, not our own selfish gratification. Or, as Martin Luther explained, "All who call on God in true faith, earnestly from the heart, will certainly be heard, and will receive what they have asked and desired."[3]

One of my favorite Bible stories about asking God for an encounter with him involves a request from a man accustomed to being ignored. Jesus was about to pass by him, so the man knew this might be his only chance. He had to ask and hold nothing back.

> Then they came to Jericho. As Jesus and his disciples, together with a large crowd, were leaving the city, a blind man, Bartimaeus (which means "son of Timaeus"), was sitting by the roadside begging. When he heard that it was Jesus of Nazareth, he began to shout, "Jesus, Son of David, have mercy on me!"
>
> Many rebuked him and told him to be quiet, but he shouted all the more, "Son of David, have mercy on me!"
>
> Jesus stopped and said, "Call him."
>
> So they called to the blind man, "Cheer up! On your feet! He's calling you." Throwing his cloak aside, he jumped to his feet and came to Jesus.
>
> "What do you want me to do for you?" Jesus asked him.
>
> The blind man said, "Rabbi, I want to see."
>
> "Go," said Jesus, "your faith has healed you." Immediately he received his sight and followed Jesus along the road.
>
> MARK 10:46–52

Can you envision this scene? A huge crowd of people has gathered. They all want a piece of Jesus — who he is, what he is doing, and "what can he do for me" kind of stuff. And in the midst of this chaos there's this blind beggar causing a scene.

The crowd must have thought he was crazy, but Bartimaeus didn't care. He will not go unnoticed. This is his opportunity to have an encounter with Jesus, the Messiah — God in the flesh! And as a result of his faith, of his unwillingness to be polite and compliant, our boy Bartimaeus experiences the supernatural healing of his sight.

We can learn a lot from Bartimaeus's encounter about how we can encounter Christ and be set free from our own blindness. I'm convinced that we, like Bartimaeus, must be *desperate for healing* before we can experience a "but God" transformation that will free us from whatever binds us.

We don't know a lot about Bartimaeus except that he was blind and a beggar. It's likely that he spent his days sitting at the side of this road. It may be that he'd been doing it for years — what kind of work could he do without his sight? "Beggar" ends up his best career option. So day after day he sat by this road, hoping for a handout. He relied on the kindness of those who passed by.

He'd heard about this Messiah. Bartimaeus couldn't see, but he heard the crowd growing larger and getting excited about ... something. He listened and realized the crowd was talking about Jesus coming by. The Son of God was going to be coming his way!

Old Bart started to get excited. This was the Jesus he had heard about! What were the odds? He started to think, *This is it! This is my chance! I've got to be heard. I'm blind, but Jesus can heal me.* Bartimaeus seemed to understand that this might be his only chance to get to someone with the power to change him. This awareness created a desperation inside of him that motivated the next few critical minutes that did indeed forever change his life.

Perhaps you identify with Bartimaeus because you too are in a place of real desperation, a place of real pain. You're bound and addicted. You're going to your computer every night, and while you tell your wife you're "working," you're clicking on all kinds of stuff that has your number. You know that you're poisoning your mind and your relationships with every new image, but you can't stop, even when you want to.

Or maybe you're struggling financially. Maybe with every paycheck, you're headed to the mall or online to shop, buying things that you hope will bring you happiness. You tell yourself excuses about why you deserve those new shoes. You justify buying yet one more thing. You try to pay your bills with what's left, but you come up short every month. You're robbing Peter to pay Paul, skipping the electricity bill this month in order to pay last month's insurance bill.

Maybe "comfort food" has a literal meaning for you as you head to the pantry or fridge every night after everyone else has gone to bed. The light from the fridge floods the dark kitchen when you open the door, and you hope desperately that no one wakes up and notices. Ice cream. Leftover pizza. A package of Oreos. You're not even hungry, but you keep eating.

You're in a place of desperation. But desperation can lead to desperate faith — Bartimaeus was desperate. He had desperate faith. This is your moment. The Messiah is real. Are you desperate enough to call out over the noise and the crowd and your addictions? The Messiah is passing right by you, just like he did with Bartimaeus. Are you willing to ask for his help?

Keep It Urgent

When this blind beggar realized that Jesus was passing by, he began to shout for him *right away*. This sense of urgency seems worth noting for us as well. In other words, *don't wait*. If you need healing, ask God to heal you right now. Bartimaeus could've continued to sit there, hoping that Jesus might notice him as he walked by. Or he could have thought, *I'm just a poor beggar. He won't hear me call out to him. And even if he did, he wouldn't stop for me.*

If any of these thoughts went through Bartimaeus's head, he tossed them aside because Scripture says, "He shouted." He was desperate! He couldn't, he wouldn't wait! He was going to ask, even in front of the large crowd. He yelled, wanting his voice to be heard above the noise of the crowd. He was doing everything he could to get the attention of Jesus.

Note too that Bartimaeus asked for healing more than once. He understood the need to *be persistent*, to do whatever it took. Bartimaeus didn't ask once and stop when Jesus didn't acknowledge him. He continued to cry out, even above the noisy roar of the crowd. They apparently didn't think he was going about getting the visiting rabbi's attention in an appropriate manner. But Bartimaeus continued to cry out until he got what he was after.

Jesus heard his cry, recognized it, and said to Bartimaeus, "What do you want me to do for you?"

Now that was worth the stick-to-itiveness. The blind beggar wanted Jesus' attention and he got it. Jesus finally asked him what he'd been aching to hear, "What can I do for you? What's your need?"

Many times, we reach the end of our rope, and we're desperate enough to call out to God to rescue us. We call out to God — once — but then we give up. Or maybe God doesn't show up for us the way we want him to. Perhaps you've heard the old joke about the guy stranded on his roof during a flood. He turns down offers to be rescued three separate times — first by someone with a life jacket, then a boat, and finally a helicopter — all because he was waiting for God to rescue him. He drowns. When the man meets God in heaven, the man complains that God didn't rescue him. God replies, "Hey, I sent you a life jacket, a boat, and a helicopter — what'd you expect?"

We have to let go of our narrow, limited expectations and open ourselves up to what God wants to do in the way he wants to do it. We have to keep asking him to notice us, to hear our prayer, to meet our need. When I say, "Be persistent," I'm not talking about ... oh, you went to church once, you prayed a time or two, you read a Bible verse. We live in a microwave society and expect everything to happen as soon as we push a button, but sometimes, you simply have to keep pushing the button. Be persistent.

I know you may have grown up in church and done the Sunday school thing. Maybe you were even in church this past week — but please realize, my friend, this is not about church attendance. This is about an encounter with God. It's about opening up your heart, opening up your mouth, opening up your soul. Paul met God while traveling. I was in a locker room. Bartimaeus was in a crowd on the side of the road. No matter where you are, God can meet you.

When you're shackled to something that won't let you go, you've got to keep going, taking the next step. Don't call out once and quit! Jesus taught, "Ask and it will be given to you; seek and you will find; knock and the door will be opened to you. For everyone who asks receives; the one who seeks finds; and to the one who knocks, the door will be opened" (Matt. 7:7 – 8).

You know you need a breakthrough. If it doesn't happen today, then get up tomorrow and ask again. Keep asking! Be persistent. Jesus will hear your cry and ask you the same question he asked Bartimaeus: *What do you want me to do for you?*

Focus on Jesus

We're shown in these verses that when Bartimaeus called out to Jesus, the crowd told him to be quiet. Maybe they didn't think a beggar had the right to call out, to shout and make a scene. Maybe they didn't want him to drown out their own cries. Maybe they were just annoyed by the noise he was making.

It can be incredibly humbling to ask God for help, to surrender to him, to admit you're desperate. Bartimaeus had been blind for years, had to beg to eat food for himself every day. The people around him didn't understand his pain; they probably didn't even try. But Bartimaeus was not fazed by their response to him. He wasn't thinking about the crowd. He was focused on Jesus, the one who could heal him.

When you need a breakthrough, you must do the same. You have to *ignore the crowd and grab hold of Jesus.*

Maybe you're going to church, sitting with your dudes, but you've been trying to keep up an image. You want to come off as that strong guy who doesn't need any help. But if you do need God's help, a breakthrough, lift your hand during worship. Your friends might think, *What is he reaching for … air?* Ignore the crowd and do it! Don't worry about what others will think. You need total surrender. You need an encounter with God.

Perhaps you're trying to come off as that cool and classy woman who has it all together. You know who you are. When your pastor says something that penetrates your heart, you tense up so no tears will smear your mascara. Sister, I'm telling you, you need a breakthrough! Let go of what others think. Let the tears flow. Quit trying to look like you're auditioning for *America's Next Top Model.* Let down your guard, let your mascara run down your cheeks, and push past that crowd.

Or maybe you're at work, getting ready for your lunch break. You know that you need to read your Bible; it's just what you need right now. But you're afraid your coworkers will think you're weird. They might call you a "holy roller" or a "Goody Two-shoes," so you leave your Bible where it is — hidden in your desk. Push past that crowd. You need help from Jesus. You are desperate and need a change. Don't worry about what the crowd thinks. You've gotta get ahold of Jesus!

Keep the Faith

We also see that Bartimaeus asked for something he believed could actually happen. He believed that Jesus could do what he asked him to do. If you want to be set free, *you gotta have faith.*

Bartimaeus does not call out to "Jesus," but calls him "Son of David," a term used to refer to the Messiah, the one who saves. The fact that Bartimaeus referred to Jesus this way shows us his belief in Christ. Use of that term also was an indication to Jesus that Bartimaeus knew who Jesus was and what he could do. Bartimaeus had faith. He believed.

Is your faith this strong? Do you believe that Jesus is who he said he is? Not just a good guy, not just a nice man, not just a popular teacher of the day, but the Messiah. If you really believe that Jesus is the Savior, then what's keeping you from calling out to him? He is the Messiah. He is the Son of God, the bright morning star. He is the Healer. He is "I Am." He's the Deliverer. He's not only the son of man, he's the Son of God. He's not just "an" answer — he is *your* answer.

Bartimaeus believed. Jesus was on his way out of town with the disciples; a huge crowd was following him. He was a popular figure in that day — people had heard about him and wanted to be close to him. So here was a large crowd, laughing, talking loudly over each other, with lots of excited noise in the area. But when Bartimaeus cried out, Jesus turned and listened. He could have kept going and no one would have noticed, but he heard Bartimaeus over the noise of the crowd and he stopped. Jesus' response is so encouraging to me! He didn't stop because of Bartimaeus's position in the church, his bank account, his good looks, his hard work, or his charming personality. The desperation in Bartimaeus's voice and his faith got Jesus' attention.

Bartimaeus told Jesus he wanted to see. He was not tentative. He was specific in his request. No sense of "Uh, you can do that, right? Do I need to go somewhere?" Bartimaeus believed. He had rock-solid faith that Jesus would give him sight. And he did. Jesus healed him right there! What a dramatic encounter with Christ. And Bartimaeus, now able to see, followed Jesus down the road.

Acknowledge Your Need

Finally, Bartimaeus reminds us to *remain humble*. He doesn't give Jesus a sob story about his life as a beggar. He doesn't justify or explain why he "deserves" healing. He doesn't whine about being a victim of circumstances and how everyone has picked on him. He doesn't claim to deserve special treatment. He simply asks for help. He makes a specific request: "I want to see."

Are you waiting until you're "good enough" to ask God for something? Are you thinking, *I gotta get clean first.* Or *I need to get out of this unhealthy relationship so I can pursue God.* The simple truth is, Jesus will begin to set you free right where you are. You don't have to be "good enough." You don't need to justify why you need help or why you deserve it. He meets us where we are, not where we should be.

When I went into that football locker room in 1992, I was far from cleaned up. I rolled up in my maroon Datsun pickup truck, cool as I could be. I went into the locker room just as I was, bound and in need of healing, but I left a completely different person.

God's grace is so amazing. We get to come to him just as we are. This can be such a hard concept for us to grasp. We live in a world where we have to earn almost everything. We're taught at a young age that if we work hard and act right, we can "earn" what we need. What grade did you get? Did you make the varsity cheerleading team? Great job, you earned it. Keep practicing and you will make the marching band. Study hard and you will make an incredible score on the ACT or SAT so you can get into college. Dress up nice for your interview so you can get the job. When you land that job, work hard to impress your boss so you can get a raise or a promotion. When you go on your date, smile, dress up, look good, and act nice.

Our entire life, we have been programmed to get ahead in life, so when we hear "Come to God just as you are," it's easy to have a little push back in your mind and think, *That's just not possible.* But it is! The Bible says that it's by grace that you've been saved, through faith, "not by works," so that no one can boast (see Eph. 2:8 – 9). Grace is God's unmerited favor. It's getting what you don't deserve. It's as crazy as someone like Bartimaeus asking a passing stranger to restore his sight.

Come As You Are

Bartimaeus came just as he was.

Paul came just as he was.

I came just as I was.

And we all encountered God, and he set us free. We all had a pivotal "but God" moment.

Do you have faith? Do you believe that if you cry out you will have an encounter with the living God that will change you forever?

In Acts 2:23 – 24, Paul explained that wicked men crucified Christ. "*But God* raised him from the dead, freeing him from the agony of death, because it was impossible for death to keep its hold on him." God raised the dead Christ so that he could be in the business of raising dead things!

The devil thought Jesus was dead. The demons were cheering. *But God* raised him from the dead!

Let me tell you what God has done and does for you: he's a God who raises dead things. You may have a dead marriage, dead career, dead relationships, dead finances, dead hope. Maybe your bondage or addiction killed these things. I'm telling you — "but God" raises from the dead! The same God who raised Jesus can set you free and revive your marriage, resuscitate your career, resurrect your relationships, replenish your finances, renew your hope, or whatever it is you need.

Come empty-handed, with nothing to offer, and in your desperation cry out to God. Listen, I can't express to you enough: I was *bound*. But I walked out of that locker room changed. I was free. There is no explanation "but God."

He's there with you right now.

He's real.

He wants to invade your life like he invaded my life all those years ago. The Scripture says, "So if the Son sets you free, you will be free indeed" (John 8:36). You can be free! You can rest in his promise. The Lord will set you free if you call out to him.

Maybe you're harboring bitterness. *But God* can change all that.

Maybe you have an addiction that no one knows about except you. *But God* can set you free.

Maybe you're stuck in the pain of a broken relationship. *But God* heals the brokenhearted.

Jesus can set you free! He responds to the prayers of desperate people. Desperate people want Jesus more than they want what Jesus has to offer. Bartimaeus didn't get a miracle and then go back to life as it was. This blind man wanted Jesus more than he wanted a miracle. After I was set free in that locker room, I embarked on the chase to know him better. I am still chasing after him. I'm still following Jesus along the road.

Whatever your situation, whatever you are struggling with, call out to the living God who can free you, who can make it possible for you to walk without being chained to something that is keeping you from the future that God has for you.

You can't do it by yourself.

But God can.

8

We're Tempted ...
But God Delivers Us

God is faithful; he will not let you be
tempted beyond what you can bear.
But when you are tempted,
he will also provide a way out
so that you can endure it.

1 CORINTHIANS 10:13

Before Tiffany and I started People's Church, I traveled as a full-time evangelist and spoke at many youth conferences across the country. If you've ever been to a youth conference, then you know the first night can be tough. That first session can be the crowd's warm-up time to get settled. The kids are dipping their toes in the water, checking the temperature. After one such slo-o-o-w-w start the first night of a youth conference, I could tell during my sermon the second night that the audience was warming up to me. I got a few good laughs (I skipped the Greek this time) and had a few points that were landing well. I felt like the teenagers' hearts were open, and God was at work in their hearts.

As I finished the message, I had everyone bow their heads. This was the time when they could respond and make a decision to live for Christ, and the response took my breath away. I just could not believe it. God had touched these kids. I watched as students flooded the aisles to get to the altar. I could see tears pouring down faces. I heard kids calling out to God — lives were being changed.

I knew the kids were responding to God, not to me. I was a willing participant, but God had somehow spoken to the youth during my sermon, and they had listened. Back in my hotel room, I felt deeply fulfilled. This was what I was made for. I flipped on the TV, changed my clothes, and called Tiffany to check in. It was great to hear her voice — it always is when I'm on the road — and as we hung up, I clicked through the channels to find ESPN. I thought I'd earned a quick SportsCenter update before bed, especially since I had to get up and prepare to preach again the next day.

That's when I saw it.

Change the Channel

A woman flashed across the screen wearing — well, to call her "scantily clad" would be overstating it. She'd need more clothes on for that to be true! I quickly pressed the arrow up button to move past that channel. But in the back of my mind, I knew there was another button that would take me back just as quickly to the not "scantily clad" woman.

Yes, I know what you're thinking. I had just preached a message about the saving blood of Jesus Christ to 2,000 students, watched them cry out at the altar and be changed by the power of God, and here I was trying to talk myself out of going back to the Non-Clothes Channel.

Shocked? Well, let me assure you, temptation likes preachers just as much as it likes you. Although God delivered me from the all-consuming power of my sexual addiction, I still face temptations. This was one of those nights.

I could have arrowed down, right back to that channel. No one would have known. There was nothing stopping me from taking that one tiny step back toward my former addiction. But God showed me the way of escape. By his grace, I did NOT go back to that channel. In fact, I knew that the smartest thing to do would be to not click through looking for ESPN. The smartest thing for me to do was to shut off the TV, and that's what I did.

I called Tiffany to clear my mind, told her what happened, and went to bed not long after. And I reminded myself of this truth: temptation is not a sin. Even Christ was tempted. If Christ was tempted, the fact that I was tempted right after I had preached the Word to all those students shouldn't be too mind-blowing. Being tempted is not a sin.

It's what you do with the temptation that matters.

And it's not an "*if, then*" situation.

It's a "*WHEN, then*" situation.

Overcoming Temptations

The apostle Paul, writing to the Corinthians, said, "So, if you think you are standing firm, be careful that you don't fall! No temptation has overtaken you except what is common to mankind" (1 Cor. 10:12 – 13). Everyone is tempted. We read in Hebrews that Jesus was tempted "in every way, just as we are — yet he did not sin" (4:15). When Christ came to earth as a man, he faced the temptations that we encounter. But because he is God, he resisted those temptations. He is the only human who has never sinned.

According to my online dictionary, if we're being "tempted" by something, then we're being "enticed or allured to do something often regarded as unwise, wrong, or immoral."[4] We don't set out to do something unwise or immoral or wrong. But we are *enticed* to do it. Temptation wraps up an immoral act in a beautiful box with a pretty bow in our favorite color. No wonder it is so hard to resist. Temptation is alluring. Appealing. Almost — and that's important to remember — irresistible. This is why Christ was the only person to ever resist temptation.

If this were the end of the story, it would be depressing. Christ was the only person to resist temptation — we're going to keep getting tempted — so where is the victory in this idea? We have to remember what Paul wrote and read the rest of that quote: "So, if you think you are standing firm, be careful that you don't fall! No temptation has overtaken you except what is common to mankind. *[But]* *God* is faithful; he will not let you be tempted beyond what you can bear. But when you are tempted, he will also provide a way out so that you can endure it" (1 Cor. 10:12 – 13, emphasis mine).

If temptation is inevitable throughout our lives, then we need to figure out how to get to the second part of that Scripture. We need to figure out how we can stand firm and experience a "but God" defense in the middle of being tempted. Because of the conviction and work of the Holy Spirit, I knew I had to turn off the TV and call Tiffany. In order to triumph over our temptations, we must allow God to work in us. We must yield to the work of his Spirit in our lives. God can and will protect us from our own sinful desires when we yield and follow the conviction and leading of the Holy Spirit. When he convicts us, we must respond.

Keeping Temptations in the Light

Because temptation thrives in darkness and secrecy, one of the primary ways we take away its power is to keep temptation in the light. As John explained, "Light has come into the world, but people loved darkness instead of light because their deeds were evil. Everyone who does evil hates the light, and will not come into the light for fear that their deeds will be exposed. But whoever lives by the truth comes into the light, so that it may be seen plainly that what they have done has been done in the sight of God" (John 3:19 – 21). When we acknowledge our weaknesses to ourselves, to God, and to other trusted people in our lives, we take temptation out of the darkness and into the light, where it can no longer thrive.

My kids are scared of the dark. Because of this irrational, yet common fear, they like to sleep with a little night-light on. This small glow usually works, and while it's not bright in their rooms like when the light's on, it's enough to let them see outlines of furniture and other things that in the dark they imagine to be scary monsters. However, my second oldest child, Cade, went through a phase where that night-light wasn't enough. Nor was his closet light. He got to the point where, for a little while, he wanted a lamp on in his room. Tiffany and I weren't going to let him, but he was not having it, and we didn't think it was too big a deal. I would turn on the lamp and kiss him on the forehead each night, watch his little body relax, and wonder how in the world he could sleep in such a bright room. "Thanks, Daddy. Now I can see what's here."

As adults, we're kind of the opposite. We're more comfortable in the dark, particularly when it comes to temptation. But if we want to resist temptation, the things that tempt us need to be lit up, exposed — to us, to God, and to those around us. We almost need to shine a figurative lamp on them to keep them in check.

Problem is, some people want only a little light. They're not scared of the dark. They've negotiated a truce with it. They've signed up for this Christian thing, but they haven't admitted that they want to dabble in some areas that they shouldn't. They just want a little night-light on. But a little light equals only a little peace.

In order to experience a "but God" moment in the

middle of being tempted, you have to become less comfortable with the dark. A lot of sin happens in the dark, whether it's in a strip club or in your dark living room with your TV or computer. You need to shine a light on whatever tempts you. Life is not a scary movie, but I want to make you afraid of the dark. In order to stand firm, you've gotta keep things in the light.

One way to keep temptation in the light is to consider the consequences of giving in to a particular temptation. "When tempted, no one should say, 'God is tempting me.' For God cannot be tempted by evil, nor does he tempt anyone; but each person is tempted when they are dragged away by their own evil desire and enticed. Then, after desire has conceived, it gives birth to sin; and sin, when it is full-grown, gives birth to death" (James 1:13 – 15). Darkness leads to sin and sin leads to death. It is no way to live.

We can try to tell ourselves that no one will know or that we're not hurting anyone, but those rationalizations simply are not true. Sin breeds destruction in our lives, in our relationships, our careers, and in our future. When we give in to temptation, it often affects not just us but also our immediate family and primary relationships. How we live our life matters.

Smoke and Fire

Maybe you've heard the old saying, "Where there's smoke, there's fire." Usually, it's used to describe a situation in which rumors foreshadow a related truth. But if temptations are smoke, then when we give in to them, we'll find ourselves in the fire. And we all know what happens then, right? It's also said that "If you play with fire, you're gonna get burned." As the great Oswald Chambers observed, "Many of us suffer from temptations from which we have no business to suffer."[5] In other words, we put ourselves in positions where we know we're vulnerable.

I'm convinced a lot of Christians play with fire. They're dabbling with things they shouldn't be messing with. They are ignoring the Spirit's voice, their spiritual GPS, and are heading down a perilous road.

For example, let's say you're married, but you're flirting with someone at work. You decide to get coffee with this person. Do I smell smoke? Then the next week you make lunch plans together. Now you're playing with fire. The outcome is predictable. As you ignore the voice of the Holy Spirit warning you to keep your distance, you tell yourself, *What's the big deal? It's just coffee. One lunch won't hurt anything. After all, he's so interesting—we're just friends.*

Or let's say you are dating a person who doesn't know the Lord. You tell yourself, "We're just dating! I wouldn't ever marry someone who wasn't a Christian!" "I can handle it!" But the reality—you can't. So you ignore the instruction of God's Word and the voice of his Spirit and keep going deeper and deeper into a close relationship with this person. Where are you headed? You might start by attending church less. Then you might begin to do other things you wouldn't expect to do because you're headed in a wrong direction.

Keeping It Real

Be honest with yourself about your weaknesses. Temptation is real. We all are all tempted, and Scripture says that Jesus is the only person who has ever been "tempted in every way," and yet "he did not sin" (Heb. 4:15). Don't lie to yourself. Give yourself a dose of reality. Don't chase after the smoke and deceive yourself into thinking you won't get burned.

If you know that you struggle with online porn, then use filters to protect yourself and to keep yourself accountable. If you're prone to overspend, then use every resource available to stick to your budget — credit counseling, budget software and apps, and expert advice. If you're likely to exaggerate the latest news you heard about someone into gossip, then find a way to keep it to yourself — or, better yet, to relay only positive comments in these situations.

Not only do you need to be real with yourself about your weaknesses, you gotta be real with God too. Don't pretend you can keep your issues in the dark with him. Instead, acknowledge that you can't live life well apart from him. Like Bartimaeus, humble yourself, and repeatedly call out to God to show you a way out of temptation, and then trust by faith that God will do what he says he will do.

Humility is essential if you want to experience a "but God" moment that will enable you to stand firm when we are being tempted. You will fail to resist every temptation if you rely on sheer willpower alone.

Matthew tells us that "the spirit is willing, but the flesh

is weak" (26:41). Left on our own, we are weak. We need to rely on God for help when we are tempted: "Because [Jesus] himself suffered when he was tempted, he is able to help those who are being tempted" (Heb. 2:18).

Christ experienced everything we struggle with — and he stood firm. Let the Holy Spirit work internally, reminding you of truth, guarding your heart, and drawing you to God. He already knows what you struggle with, even before you do. You can't keep secrets from him. God wants you to have the faith that he will help you resist when you are tempted to sin.

Here's how the psalmist explained our need to turn to God during these situations: "My flesh and my heart may fail, *but God* is the strength of my heart and my portion forever" (Ps. 73:26, emphasis mine). When we are real with God about our temptations and keep them in the light with him, we allow him to be our strength when we are at our weakest moments.

In addition to being real with yourself and with God, you also gotta be real with others. Find reliable, trustworthy believers with whom you can share your struggles, temptations, and, yes, those times when you give in to temptation. Regardless of the particular struggles we face, we must tell someone we trust about our areas of vulnerability. We all need other people to keep us accountable. Too often we keep the people around us in the dark because it would be too embarrassing to admit that we don't "have it all together." But God brings his church, other believers, into our lives so that we can live in freedom.

If people knew you struggled with certain things,

what would they think of you? What would your small group think if they knew that you're constantly thinking of ways to cheat the boss at work, from the time card to the petty cash drawer? You may not actually be doing it, but the point is that it is a huge temptation for you that takes up a lot of your thought time. You've got to talk to someone about these temptations and let yourself be accountable to that person. And remember — accountability is only as good as your commitment level to it. Be real. When we allow ourselves to be held accountable by someone, we are no longer hiding and we are more likely to have victory over temptation. Remember, things grow in the dark, when hidden. We must bring our weaknesses into the light so we experience victory.

What would your friend think if she knew that you regularly struggle with jealousy toward her? Even though you sometimes realize how ridiculous your jealousy is, the first thing that pops into your head when you see her is how you wish you had her clothes or you wish you were liked the way people seem to adore her. You're jealous. It's leading to resentment and bitterness, and you're not talking to anyone about it. Now I'm not saying you should talk to your friend about it. But you do need to tell someone who can counsel you and who will pray for you.

James reminds us to "confess your sins to each other and pray for each other so that you may be healed. The prayer of a righteous person is powerful and effective" (5:16). Note the word *righteous*. The person who holds you accountable needs to be a righteous person who is living for God. This means you can't go to Shaniqua and complain together about your friend with the clothes.

That is gossip, not confession. Bring your struggle into the light of confession, pray about it with someone, and set up trusted accountability.

Maybe you are one of the many men who struggle with the temptation of pornography. Alluring images bombard you on a daily basis. Even the ads on billboards or the scantily clad women on magazine covers at the supermarket are a draw for you. You try to avert your eyes and shut out the temptation, but it's a huge struggle for you every single day. You know it. But how do you talk about it? Your wife would just die if she knew. It's not the type of conversation you've ever had with her. How would you even bring it up? What would she assume about the way you feel about her?

If you want to walk in victory — you have to get some accountability partners. This has been incredibly helpful and freeing for me. I've got a couple guys I'm raw with, and I tell them when I'm tempted. And most importantly, I've had several talks with Tiffany about the areas of my life where I'm tempted. She is not "in the dark" about these areas, and because of that, she can pray for me and help me make smart decisions in that area. I brought this temptation out into the light, and because of that, it is easier for me to resist areas of temptation.

Get into the Word

You've had an encounter with Christ. You had a "but God" moment where he set you free, and you are changed. But you still face the same old temptations. They don't just disappear, which means you must make the decision every day to follow Christ.

So how else can you stand firm in your faith when you are tempted?

You can replace the things that tempt you with better options. I'm talking about actually changing the way your brain thinks. Don't assume that your brain is just neutral. It can be a weapon against you or a tool to assist you. The input of what goes into your mind is crucial. Romans 12:2 tells us to "be transformed by the renewing of your mind." This transformation doesn't happen by accident. We have to make a decision to replace our old way of thinking with thoughts about God.

So *get yourself into the Word.* The Bible is your best defense against sin; truth trumps temptation every time. We see this in how Jesus resisted Satan when he tempted him. Every time Satan suggested a temptation, Jesus quoted Scripture. The tempter told the famished Messiah to turn the stones into bread, but Jesus quoted Deuteronomy to him: "Man does not live on bread alone but on every word that comes from the mouth of the LORD" (8:3). Next, the devil tried to get Jesus to demonstrate his power by showing off, and the Lord responded by quoting Deuteronomy 6:16, an admonition against testing God. Finally, the enemy offers Christ the world on a platter to which Jesus answers, "Fear the LORD your God, serve him only" (6:13).

You won't be able to wield God's truth against temptation if you don't know what the Bible says about specific topics. So read the Word, study it, read commentaries, go to Bible studies, and, like Psalm 119:11 says, hide God's words in your heart so that you won't sin against him.

The more you renew your mind with the Word, the further you push the darkness away. His Word is a lamp for your feet and a light on your path (Ps. 119:105).

There are all kinds of Bible studies available at bookstores, many good and free studies available online, and an app for smartphones called YouVersion. It is free, contains the whole Bible, and it can help set you up on a Bible reading plan. Your phone will remind you every day. You can even listen to the Bible on this app if reading is not your thing.

God's Word can cut through the self-justifications and the enemy's accusations that fly through your mind. Earlier in the book I revealed my struggles with insecurity. When battling self-doubts, I often recalled God's truth that I'm "fearfully and wonderfully made" (Ps. 139:14), and it made a huge difference. That verse alone got me through some struggles with the temptation to doubt myself.

I also renewed my mind by filling it with pure and positive thoughts about Christ. Philippians tells us, "Whatever is pure ... lovely ... think about such things" (4:8). Instead of dwelling on seductive images, I learned to focus on the joy I experience in following Jesus and the peace I enjoy when loving my wife with integrity. When we renew our minds with God's truth, it does wonders in helping us to stand firm in our faith.

Talk with God Every Day

If you want to stand firm in your faith, it's critical that you spend time with the Lord in prayer every single day.

Why every day? Isn't God powerful enough to take on our problems if we talk to him, say, three days a week?

Yes, but it's not about what God is capable of doing. It is about us. We need to be renewed and reminded every single day. We need to talk with our Father and share all that's going on with us. Spending time with the Lord and getting to know him will lessen the power of your temptations simply because your desire for them will diminish. When you experience "but God" contentment, then the counterfeit comforts offered by sinful temptations lose their appeal.

Daily prayer may be a new practice for you. Maybe you have no idea what you would even say for very long. Maybe you're tired of praying the way you think you're supposed to pray. Remember, God just wants you to talk to him. He already knows all your weaknesses, struggles, and flaws. He knows what will tempt you before you ever encounter it. He wants to protect you and draw you close. Deliverance from temptation comes when you rely on him, trust his Word, listen to his voice, and follow his leading, rather than your own ways.

Preventive Measures

In order to resist temptations, it helps to make a plan for how we will respond when confronted with temptations. "But God" victories result when we establish preventive measures that help us to immediately remove ourselves from tempting situations without wavering or thinking through what you need to do. After all, why set yourself up for failure?

Here are some of the safeguards that Tiffany and I have established to make it difficult for either of us to succumb to temptations that might harm our marriage:

- We are not alone with the opposite sex — ever, for any reason.
- We don't have "friends" of the opposite sex that we talk with on the phone, private message on Facebook, or text. We text regarding only work-related things and usually include one another on those texts.
- We have blocked half the channels on our television (the "dirty" half!).
- I make every effort not to travel alone.
- I make every effort not to stay in a hotel room alone. I take Tiffany, one of my kids, or a male staff member.
- I can access the Internet, Twitter, or Facebook only through X3watch, a safety filter on my phone.
- I have a filter on my computer. Tiffany and a staff member receive a report every month on my search history. I know they will see everything I've searched for and visited.

We have other safeguards, but you get the idea. Some people find out how we live and think that we're extreme, but you've got to be extreme when dealing with a former addiction and current temptations.

Everybody is tempted differently. What kind of safeguards do you need on your life? Maybe it's time for you to get that filter for your computer. Maybe you need to cut up your credit cards so you stop overspending. Maybe you need to take a different route home so you don't keep driving past the place where you always got drinks after work.

Everybody thinks they can beat the odds. "I'm strong enough — I'll be okay. I can handle it. We're just talking. (In a dark car. Alone. In close proximity.) We're just talking! I can handle it!" But a lot of times, we want to handle temptation ourselves because we want to get as close to it as possible without crossing the line. That is a dangerous game to play.

As you sift through the many decisions you have to face every day, God wants you to use wisdom and heed the voice of his Spirit. Scripture tells us that there are some things that are *permissible* for us to do that are not necessarily *beneficial* (1 Cor. 10:23). Remember, just because it is permissible for you to have dinner with someone from work, that doesn't mean it's beneficial for you to do. If you are married and this dinner companion is not your spouse, is this dinner date going to get you where you're trying to go? It's important that we use wisdom, turn on our "floodlights," and establish some preventive measures.

What are your weaknesses? Take a minute, be real, and answer. Now, what kind of safeguards do you need to establish?

Parents, do you need to establish some preventive measures for your kids? I can only imagine what I would have done with today's technology when I was a kid. My parents shouldn't have trusted me, despite my good grades and athlete status. Remember how creative I was at sneaking girls in and out of my parents' house? You might never do something as crazy as build a garage onto your son's bedroom and create an easy escape for him. You may have thought that was stupid when you read my story about my sneaking out. But when was the last time you checked your kids' cell phones? How often are you doing a history of your son's search engine on his computer? Safeguards prevent accidents from happening.

Living in Freedom

Maybe you're thinking, *I thought this chapter was about living free. How am I supposed to be free if I'm having all these boundaries all over my life?* Living free is not about following a bunch of rules. It's about being real and making wise decisions so you can live in freedom, without worry.

Temptation finds its way to every single person. I'm not immune. Neither are you. You may feel great the day you're reading this chapter. You may feel confident that you can get around without your light. But here's what I know: Everybody has a bad day. And if on your bad day you don't have your safeguards in place, it is much easier to fail than to succeed.

Jesus came to earth so that we not only can live, but live life to the full. This doesn't mean that life in Christ equals life without problems or temptations. But God promises to strengthen us and empower us to resist temptation. "But the Lord is faithful, and he will strengthen you and protect you from the evil one" (2 Thess. 3:3).

Please understand that no matter how much darkness you have in your life or what you have done, God can handle it and lead you out of it. *"God is light"* (1 John 1:5, emphasis mine). In him, there is no darkness. And he is ready to put his light onto your situation, whatever it is.

Temptation will happen. But God can make you stronger than any enticement you face.

9

We Don't Have Enough ...
But God Provides for Us

*And my God will meet all your needs according
to the riches of his glory in Christ Jesus.*

PHILIPPIANS 4:19

Maybe you've had an initial "but God" experience, but now find yourself doubting his ability to love you, to provide for you, to rescue you, to intervene for you. You feel like you never have enough of what you need, that you're never enough for what life requires. You're burned out, tired, and resigned to a mediocre life.

You don't have to stay that way.

While it's true that on your own you will never have enough of what you need, God has more than enough —daily bread to sustain you, assurance and support to strengthen you, and the presence of his Spirit to encourage and empower you. No matter where you are in life, if you're battered and broken by life, God can mend you. He can restore you. He can redeem even the most painful experiences in your life.

Will you let him?

If you are skeptical about how a "but God" encounter can transform your worst moments into the seeds for your divine destiny, then read on. I want to share my all-time favorite story of God's ability to transform every area of our lives. One woman embodies almost all the "but God" principles we've been talking about and illustrates how you can draw strength, insight, hope, and encouragement from your relationship with God, even in the darkest, most painful challenges. From unbearable loss, this woman experienced unbelievable blessing.

If you remain unsure about how to experience God's redemptive power in every area of your life, then I pray this story will bring clarity and inspiration. If you're already identifying God's faithfulness, provision, and grace in your life, then I pray this woman's example will encourage you to keep running the race.

Unbearable Loss

Imagine a woman who has been married to the love of her life for years. They have followed the Lord faithfully and built a satisfying life together. They have two sons. They take little getaways to Lake Israel when time allows, and they remain faithful to each other. She depends on the love of her life and trusts him as the sole provider.

Then one day, everything changes. Her heart is ripped into pieces as her husband, friend, confidant, lover, and father of her children is unexpectedly taken from her by death. The loss of her husband feels almost unbearable. And she realizes she has to somehow muster up the strength to tell her two sons. With tears in her eyes, she calls her two sons to come sit next to her. Looking them in the eyes, she says, "Boys, your dad died this morning in an accident." Her two boys can hardly grasp what she is telling them, but as it begins to sink in, they start to wail, intensifying the pain she is already experiencing. She pulls them close into her arms, and they all mourn together.

Time seems to pass so slowly. As she holds her boys, she is overwhelmed with deep grief and cries out to God, *Why! Why is this happening? You know I need my husband! You know my boys need their dad! You know I don't have the strength to raise these boys by myself! You know I can't provide for them by myself! God, why?*

The next day she wakes up with a heavy heart and starts to make funeral arrangements. Someone knocks on the door of her home. Expecting to see a family member who's come to comfort her, she sees instead a stranger standing there when she opens the door. It's an imposing man who snarls at her, "Your husband owes us $10,000. You have until the end of the week."

"But I don't have $10,000!" she protests. "My husband just died. There is no way —"

"Save your sob story. Doesn't change the facts. You can't pay? We'll take your two sons."

The man turns to leave, and she lunges after him.

"Please! Don't take my kids! Please, sir! They are all I have left!" She's hysterical.

She falls to the ground and screams out to God. *First you take my husband away from me! And now you're going to take my kids!*

Things could not be worse.

Rope of Redemption

These were good people. But being good did not exclude them from a terrible tragedy. They loved the Lord, they served him, and still the life they had built together fell apart.

When difficult situations happen, how does anyone find the strength to go on? It's hard to think about emotional healing when you're numb with grief and overwhelmed by what the future holds — more loss, more pain, more sorrow, as if one loss leads to another. And yet so often this is the way life happens. We suffer a setback, and suddenly we feel like the snowball we just dodged has turned into an avalanche. We end up feeling alone, wondering how we can keep going.

The truth is, you can't do it alone. You have to be as resourceful as you can be, but you have to ask for help. You must trust God for something that you may not even be able to imagine or put into words. That's what happened with this poor woman. She thought she was at the end of her rope, but God turned her rope into a redemptive lifeline to the future that he had ready for her. Let's take a look.

The wife of a man from the company of the prophets cried out to Elisha, "Your servant my husband is dead, and you know that he revered the LORD. But now his creditor is coming to take my two boys as his slaves."

Elisha replied to her, "How can I help you? Tell me, what do you have in your house?"

"Your servant has nothing there at all," she said, "except a small jar of olive oil."

Elisha said, "Go around and ask all your neighbors for empty jars. Don't ask for just a few. Then go inside and shut the door behind you and your sons. Pour oil into all the jars, and as each is filled, put it to one side."

She left him and shut the door behind her and her sons. They brought the jars to her and she kept pouring. When all the jars were full, she said to her son, "Bring me another one."

But he replied, "There is not a jar left." Then the oil stopped flowing.

She went and told the man of God, and he said, "Go, sell the oil and pay your debts. You and your sons can live on what is left."

2 KINGS 4:1–7

Notice this poor woman's response in the midst of devastating tragedy. She immediately told someone who shared her faith in God. In fact, she chose to run to the man closest to God at the time, his prophet Elisha. If there was going to be help from the Lord, then Elisha was the go-to guy who could tell you how it would happen.

Keep in mind, though, that this woman didn't know

how her story was going to end. For all she knew, Elisha might've told her to buzz off and leave him alone. Maybe he wouldn't have been unkind about it, but she had no guarantees. If anything, going to him was a long shot.

But it was her only shot. And when you're up against a wall, you do what you have to do. You do whatever you *can* do.

This woman could've easily sat inside her home, too frightened, too vulnerable to try to find help. She was powerless. She could have blamed God and played the victim — or, better yet, the martyr. After all, wasn't she doing everything in her power to follow God, and this was what she got? If that didn't make everyone admire her faith and feel sorry for her, then nothing would!

But this woman, in her desperation, "cried out" to Elisha for help: "Please ... just listen. My husband, your servant, is dead. His creditor is coming to take my two boys. Please, I need help."

She does not try to overcome her challenges on her own. She doesn't try to save face or pretend that everything is okay. She doesn't try to act like she has it all together while she's falling apart. She understands all too clearly that she needs help. She needs to tell someone. Ask for help. There was only one thing to do.

Weathering the Storm

Not only does she ask for help, but she listens closely to what God says through the prophet Elisha, then follows his instructions exactly as they were said to her. She could have thought his instructions to fill each big jar to the top with oil from her little jar didn't make sense. She had so little oil. She didn't question the instructions or argue. Instead, in her desperation, she was willing to do whatever it took to save her sons.

Like Bartimaeus, she knew that desperate times call for desperate measures. She didn't stop and second-guess Elisha or look ahead and consider how scientifically impossible it would be for her little dab of oil to fill every empty vessel in her neighborhood. Humbled by her tragic circumstances, she followed her request for help by being obedient to the instructions she was given. She did what she was told to do, without question and without hesitation.

Do you want to receive God's healing power? Do you want to let go of your past and your hurt? Do you want to enter into the abundant life that God has for you? Then you've got to get to a place where you're willing to allow God's Word to work in you. You've got to be willing to ask his people for assistance. You've got to be willing to do what you know you can do. You've got to get to a place where you are willing to do whatever it takes.

What do you need to do — *right now, today* — in order to allow God's presence into your problem? How do you feel about what you need to do in order to seek God's power in the midst of your problems?

When we stifle our emotions and try to handle everything by ourselves, we hinder our progress and miss out on a "but God" encounter. Bottling our emotions prevents us from acknowledging our need, our limitations, our desperation, and it definitely makes it harder to ask for help. Learning how to express our emotions as we turn to our Father for help allows us to be humble, open, and vulnerable.

God's Word gives us a ton of wisdom on how to manage our emotions. One example is in Ephesians: " 'In your anger do not sin': Do not let the sun go down while you are still angry" (4:26). What God doesn't do is tell us to *deny* our emotions.

The danger of keeping our major losses to ourselves is that we don't get input or help from any other healthy sources. Instead we keep beating ourselves up in our heads or telling ourselves lies, exaggerating what has happened by imagining the worst possible consequences. We lose perspective, often getting farther and farther from the truth.

Mark Twain wisely observed, "Life does not consist mainly — or even largely — of facts and happening. It consists mainly of the storm of thoughts that are forever blowing through one's mind."[6] The storms of life will pass. Even though it feels like there is no calm eye in the midst of the raging winds around us, God provides shelter when we turn to him. Even though it feels like our lives are over, "but God" can transform them if we follow his guidance.

When we turn to him — through his Word and his people — we gain not just objectivity but clarity and a supernatural perspective. We begin to see things from God's viewpoint. When life beats us up, we have to tell those who care about us. We have to get a true perspective.

Maybe you're facing an enormous loss that leaves you with a variety of conflicting emotions — fear, anger, hurt, doubt, anxiety. Maybe it's a secret from your past or a burden of worry about the future. Maybe you're concerned about your reputation and others' perceptions of you, so you keep your need to yourself and try to hold your life together. By yourself. Alone.

But God wants you to know you don't have to. You're not alone. And you can be healed. I'm living proof of that, along with millions of other people around the world. Lay down your burden. Tell someone you trust and respect for their relationship with God. You may feel like your jar has been shattered and can't be fixed, but God wants to restore the pieces and fill you with healing.

Daily Bread

God always meets us where we are, each day, and asks only that we depend on him. I'm convinced this is the essence of the "daily bread" that Jesus instructs us to ask for when we pray. We simply ask for what we need right now and allow God to take care of the future.

So often we reduce "give us this day our daily bread" to our immediate physical needs — especially basics like food. But there's a spiritual, emotional, and even mental aspect to daily bread. We need to ask God to meet our spiritual needs each day as well. Sometimes we're worried about next week's groceries, next month's paycheck, or next year's budget when we really need to focus on today. Your daily bread today might be just having the emotional strength to get through this *one* day. On really hard days, maybe it's the ability just to get through the next hour. Whatever we need to be able to take the next step, God will provide for us.

Our friend the widow certainly knew that she had to take things moment by moment, step by step. Elisha asked her, "What do you have in your house?" to which she replied, "Your servant has nothing there at all" — and then, almost as an afterthought — "except a little oil."

It may have seemed strange to her that Elisha would ask her what *she* had when she was the one who went to him for help. She may have been thinking, *Why do you ask me? I'm a widow. I'm broke! I have nothing! Except for a small amount of oil, and that's going to be used up in a few days. They will take my sons!*

Consider what she was facing: A grieving widow with two sons and no money to buy food or pay what the man said she owes. What she has isn't enough. What she has can't take care of her boys. What she has cannot protect her sons from the harm that's about to come to them. All she has is a little oil. Too little to help.

It was "nothing ... except a little oil" to this widow, this mom, who was about to lose even her sons. But that small amount of oil was enough. God used the widow's remaining bit of oil to fill jars and jars to the brim with valuable olive oil, enough for her to pay the debt with enough left over for her and her two sons to live off of for the rest of her life. She was faithful. She did exactly what was asked, and God filled not only the jars she had but *all* the empty jars she could gather from neighbors. That "little oil" she had was the catalyst to her miracle.

You see, God doesn't perform miracles with what we don't have; he performs miracles using the little that we do have. We see what we have as not being enough, but in

God's hands, our resources, no matter how small or how few, are more than enough. Little becomes much when God gets ahold of it.

I have seen this over and over in my life. When Tiffany and I moved to Oklahoma City in 2002, I was 26 and she was 24. We had never been lead pastors before. Okay, we had never even been on a church staff before! We were naive and inexperienced. We were young compared to the average age of most lead pastors. You know we were inexperienced because we held the grand opening of our church on Mother's Day! We didn't realize that on Mother's Day, most people attend their mom's or grand-mother's church. We also didn't think through that two weeks later was Memorial Day and the end of the school year, the gateway to summer, a time when some people take a break from church. We didn't know any of that.

At our grand opening, we started with 65 people and quickly went backwards. I was introverted, inexperi-enced, and insecure. I began to wonder if we had missed God's message to us. I wondered if our brand-new church would make it. I wondered if I was supposed to lead this new church. I didn't have much to offer God, but just like the widow, I decided to give my insecure, introverted, and inexperienced self to God. I prayed, *Lord, here are my empty jars. Here's our church. I don't know what I'm doing, but I place it all in your hands.*

God began to fill my jars by bringing great pastors and leaders, like Craig Groeschel, around me to provide wis-dom, guidance, and encouragement. God began to take the little I had to offer and to multiply it. By August 2002, we had our first Sunday with more than a hundred people — and we never dipped below that milestone. I gave what I had, and God transformed it into what he wanted.

He can turn your little bit of oil into many jars full of oil too. Whatever your struggle, God can turn it into your strength — and a place from which to minister to others. Sometimes our willingness to change is the little dab of oil that God uses to meet our needs.

Maybe you're struggling financially, deep in debt or in bankruptcy. With God's power, you can become a dedicated steward who learns from past mistakes. You may feel like you don't have the quality relationships you need to help you fulfill your God-given dreams and priorities, just lots of social media connections. But God can transform your regular relationships into divine connections that transform your life and your future. The widow experienced a divine connection through the prophet Elisha that helped her fulfill her God-given dreams and priorities — to save her sons from slavery and to provide for them.

God provides divine connections to meet our needs and to fulfill his plans for our lives. Whatever it is that you're struggling with, if you turn it over to God, he can not only overcome your problem but transform it. You need only a little bit of faith. A little bit of trust.

We have only a little, but God has a lot.

Ask the Right People

As the widow's story demonstrates, our relationships have an enormous impact on fulfilling our divine destiny. When we're in need, when we're faced with impossible circumstances or painful challenges, God provides the right people for us. But to recognize them, we must stop focusing just on our situation, our problem, and look around us for the people God has already brought on the scene and focus on the ones who can provide what we need.

Imagine what would have happened if the widow had gone to the wrong person. Imagine that instead of asking Elisha, she asked someone she happened to run into, who turned out to be good old Joe, who has some special *ideas* on how she can make money. Joe tells her, "You know, Naomi has a little scheme going where she's making lots of money. Now, she does some stuff I can't talk about — unless you are serious. Really need help. I know you're a respectable woman and all, but desperate times call for desperate measures. Naomi fell on desperate times, but now that girl's got it goin' on. It might seem scandalous to some people, but I'm just saying. If you wanna keep them two boys of yours and keep that roof over your head, you might have to get a little scandalous."

Laugh if you want (well, I sort of hope you did), but seriously, the people we go to when we need help determine our ability to access God's provision. Why would we go to people who don't know God to ask for something that only God can provide? We should never risk entrusting our needs to someone who could lead us down a road that dishonors God and his Word.

The widow could have been in a very different situation with only horrible options, but she and her husband clearly had developed a relationship with the right person, the right friendship. (Remember what I said earlier? *Show me your friends and I'll show you your future*.) Elisha was a man of God. Elisha was a powerful prophet. He was a wise man. She was already aware of Elisha's status and somehow had access to him. And when this widow fell on hard times, this relationship gave her the opportunity for a "but God" provision. The right people can facilitate "but God" encounters just as the wrong people can eliminate them.

The widow's "but God" moment happened because she humbled herself and sought help from Elisha, whom God had already placed in her life. Elisha tells her what to do — gather a lot of jars and fill them with oil from her small jar. In obedience, she does what he tells her to do. She once again swallows her pride and asks her neighbors for their empty jars. Elisha had told her, "Don't ask for just a few" (2 Kings 4:3). God blesses her actions. She collects all the jars she will need.

I can see one of her neighbors who knows her well, knew her husband, saying, "Of course I will help you! I can't believe what's happened to you! I don't have any money, but here, I've been saving up these jars to store my vegetables from my garden. You take them. I have a lot, so it may take you several trips. Take them all."

We feel like we're struggling alone, but God reminds us that we need other people, and he opens the door for these "but God" relationships.

Panic to Prosperity

When her husband died and everything she knew changed, the widow didn't just wait for something else to happen. She took action. She went for help.

By acknowledging her need and turning to God (and his people) for help, she discovered that the little she had was more than enough. She could have drowned in her despair, but God offered a lifeline of provision and hope. Her panic became her prosperity. She went from being helpless to seeing a whole new future unveiled. God intervened and made a way for the impossible to happen.

We can't use logic or science to explain it; 2 + 2 does not equal 4 in this equation. The widow took the small amount of oil she had and filled and filled and filled jar after jar after jar. She filled up so many jars that she had enough oil to not only pay off the debt but also to live on for the rest of her life. Don't try to explain it! You can't! It was a supernatural experience. What might've seemed like an exercise in futility became an encounter with the divine provision of God.

Faith to Persevere

I understand that it's much easier to make excuses, to justify your uncertainty, to linger with your doubts. The widow had plenty of opportunities to say, "I'm just doing the best I know how to do. I'm done. Life is over. This is it."

But she wanted to change.

She hoped for change.

She didn't give up. She didn't succumb to self-pity or

despair. No — something stirred in her and said, "Things can be different. I don't know how, but I know they can be. I'm not gonna give up. I'm just not." Some little tiny mustard seed of hope spurred her toward faith.

She was not willing to keep doing the same thing. Unfortunately many people are. They have determined that they've already tried everything, that they're doing the best they can and there's nothing left to do. They're basically saying, "I'm not gonna go to the prophet and ask for help." Which leads to "I'm not gonna go to the neighbors to ask them for help either." Which then becomes, "I'm a failure. A loser. No one can help me get out of this mess."

They never reach that "but God" moment because they never turn to God. They stick with what they know, no matter how painful and self-defeating those things are.

The widow's tenacity, her push through, her refusal to give up brought her to her "but God" moment and the change in her life.

The widow could have lost her sons ... *but God.* She could have lived flat broke the rest of her life ... *but God.* She could have suffered from depression the rest of her life ... *but God.* She could have been too emotionally distraught after her husband died to go to the prophet ... *but God!*

But God changes everything! Believe it! Live it!

Too many people don't have a "but God" moment because they have lost all hope. They lack knowledge, patience, and perseverance. They have no faith to make that move to God. They aren't willing to "go and get the jars." They fixate on what they see as impossible and give up.

But the widow knew a secret. She knew that to have hope she would have to let go of knowing for sure what would happen and just do what the wise man told her to do. No questions, no arguments, no putting it off until later. So many people lose all hope because they can't figure out how to solve their problem. So they do nothing. They just wait and thereby miss out on what God wants to use to solve their problems and meet their needs.

Our perception of what seems likely, possible, feasible, probable, or realistic is limited. But God isn't limited by what we can comprehend.

With God all things are possible.

10

We See Impossible ...
But God Makes
All Things Possible

Jesus looked at them and said, "With man this is impossible, but with God all things are possible."

MATTHEW 19:26

My friends Bob and Karen had been saving for years so they could finally go on a real vacation alone together. (I teased Bob more than his wife about how their three-night honeymoon at the Howard Johnson down the street didn't count.) They married young, started having kids soon after, and lived bare bones as Bob worked his entry-level job at the power plant. Eventually, after a few raises and a few more years, they had saved enough money to go on a nice vacation that would double as a makeup honeymoon.

Karen found what they both considered a good deal through a reputable online travel site. They booked a resort in the Caribbean, scheduled their flight, and counted the days until they dropped the kids off with Karen's sister and took their first-ever real vacation.

The trip started by being everything they had hoped it would be. The weather was perfect. Postcard perfect, the beautiful Caribbean beach glistened as turquoise water kissed white sands. Karen couldn't believe she was actually taking a vacation in such a beautiful place — it felt like a dream!

Bob was impressed too, but couldn't enjoy it quite as much as he'd hoped. It was hard to get away from worrying about the amount of money they were spending. The restaurants were so much more expensive than they were at home — a lot more than he'd budgeted — so they tried to make up for it by doing fewer activities. They steered toward the pool and the beach as much as possible. No shopping or souvenir hunting.

Karen didn't seem to mind, but as they packed up on the last day, Bob feared that she was disappointed. He dreaded getting their next credit-card bills. He'd tried to shield her from the totals that seemed to multiply every time she ordered a Coke or one of those fruity little non-alcoholic drinks with the umbrellas. As they were about to leave for the airport to return home, Bob mentally calculated how much overtime he would need to work to make up for the unforeseen extra money they'd spent.

They stopped by the front desk to check out, and the

hotel associate chatted with Bob and asked how they had enjoyed their stay. Bob answered politely enough, and then the young man asked, "Did you enjoy our selection of restaurants? Would you mind filling out a survey?"

"I'm sorry, we didn't eat here this week," Bob told him. He didn't want to say why — that the restaurants at the hotel looked too fancy and expensive. No point in telling him that they had found a Subway for lunch most days and some different restaurants in the evenings, and even these were too expensive.

The hotel clerk looked quizzically at Bob, then started clicking on the computer.

"Uh, sir … you and your wife booked an *all-inclusive* vacation here. That means that all of your meals were included with your stay. Yet it appears that you didn't eat with us even once. I hope you'll reconsider and try our food on your next visit."

Bob had missed a few important details when they booked their vacation. The fine print. And their lack of knowledge caused them to miss out on a huge benefit. A huge loss.

Making Excuses

I know this story sounds crazy. In this day and age, with everyone trying to stretch their dollar as far as it can go, who would book a vacation without knowing what is included? But hold that thought. Even though we're constantly bombarded with information, we often become overwhelmed and fail to comprehend all that we're told. And some of the information we miss could improve our life in dramatic ways — much more than just free buffets and endless refills by the pool.

You see, some of us go through life without knowing what blessings are available to us — without knowing or believing what can actually be "included." Scripture warns us, "My people are destroyed from lack of knowledge" (Hosea 4:6). It's no accident that "destroyed" used here is a strong word — it means to suffer destruction or spiritual death. So without knowledge, we can find ourselves in the middle of destruction or even our own spiritual death. Obviously, considering such an ominous definition, you immediately wonder, "What knowledge am I lacking? How do I get it?"

As a pastor, I've noticed that some people lack the knowledge and understanding that *real change is possible*. No matter what you've done, what you haven't done that you think you should have, or what others have done to you — you can change. I know, as a pastor I'm supposed to say something like this. But it's true.

Maybe you're thinking, *Well, I've tried to change — I really have. But I ... just ... couldn't.* Maybe you're thinking of how you tried to lose weight or quit smoking. You know, something like, "Sure, I *tried* going on a diet. More than once. I tried a lot. It didn't work." Or, "I stopped smoking for about three weeks. But then I got stressed out at work and ... it just didn't stick." Maybe it's your default reaction that you've tried to alter: "I was doing really good not yelling at my kids, and then Jimmy lied to me, and I flew off the handle."

And you know what? You're right. *You will never change by your own power.*

We can't change ourselves, but God can transform us.

Unfortunately, many people struggle with this truth, not allowing it to seep into the fiber of their being. They might even believe it as a concept or scriptural truth, but they don't think it applies to them. Instead of experiencing the transformative power of a "but God" encounter, they use "but God" to make excuses for their lack of faith and lack of action. Much like a child might say, "But *MOM!* I'm tired. I don't want to clean my room!" Or "But *Da-ad!* You don't understand! Everyone else is going! Why can't I?" They say:

"But God, I can't do that! Look at my past!"

"But God, my marriage is beyond repair."

"But God, my teenager is strung out on drugs."

"But God, I've got $50,000 of credit-card debt."

"But God, I've been addicted for *twenty* years."

"But God, I've tried everything. I'm afraid this might just be who I am — or at least who I'm going to be."

If any of these sound familiar to you, remember, you can't change — but GOD can change you! He changes everything. Don't let "but God" be a preface for your excuses. Instead, allow God to change what seems impossible into a reminder of his power, glory, and love for you.

Keep Hope Alive

The cross isn't just about your sins being forgiven. It is about the fact that you CAN change. Not "but God, I can't." Instead you can proclaim, "But God, thank you,

Lord, YES, I can!" You have a new identity through the power of Jesus' death and resurrection. This means the way you've been living is not something you have to continue doing. Your lifestyle may have gotten you through hard times for a while, but now God is on your side. That first "but God" encounter begins a chain reaction of other "but God" transformations in your life.

Because of this fact, there's hope. Because of Christ, because of his resurrection, you *can* change your situation, whether it is finances, career, marriage, or other relationships. Real, tangible, visible change can happen!

When you begin to realize this, something happens inside you. All of a sudden you find yourself saying, "I don't want to be this way anymore." You begin to see that the life you are living isn't the life you have to keep on living. And certainly not the life you were created to live. This understanding becomes the catalyst for thoughts like, *I can't stay in this abusive relationship anymore. I don't want to settle for my health being like this the rest of my life.* Like me, you might decide, *I don't want to live my life like* this!"

The good news is you don't have to. You can change. God can show up in the middle of your desperate situation. You can find every open door leading to change. Your future can look different than your past looks.

My life is a living example of how a life changes *completely* because of God. It all began with that initial "but God" encounter, the change in my life's direction that put me in alignment with the Creator's plans for my life.

Keep Doing Your Part

I know you've tried willpower. But it's not enough. You've got to BELIEVE change is possible. And you've got to make the move. Take the first step. You've got to do your part. Whether it's building an ark, standing up to a giant, or getting your jars for oil, you have to do what you can. Go to that counseling session with your spouse. Figure out a way to spend some quality time with your kid who's been rebelling. Cut up the credit cards. Get out of the unhealthy dating relationship. Stop going to that place where you wind up going home with someone you just met. Tell someone you trust and respect what's going on so that they will check in on you and hold you accountable.

Do what you can do.

Have you convinced yourself that you can't change? That maybe even God can't change you? You're wrong. That is simply not true. Your thinking is distorted. You need to renew your mind! You gotta start seeing yourself the way God sees you — start believing what he says about you. Consider some of the truths we've touched on throughout these pages:

- But God showed his great love for us by sending Christ to die for us while we were still sinners (Rom. 5:8 NLT).

- No, in all these things we are more than conquerors through him who loved us (Rom. 8:37).

- I praise you because I am fearfully and wonderfully made; your works are wonderful, I know that full well (Ps. 139:14).

If you want to exchange your "stinkin' thinkin'" for God's truth, then you know what you have to do: Get into the Word and get some perspective. Hide those inspirational words in your heart to replace the negative. Have faith that God can change you. Absorb the truth.

Or maybe you have the knowledge but lack the faith. You just can't bring yourself to take action and do what God asks you to do. So you are frustrated and stuck. You even come up with a way to blame God, the very One who wants to show up in your life and make a difference. When Jesus went to his hometown, the Bible tells us he "could not do any miracles there, except lay his hands on a few sick people and heal them. He was amazed at their lack of faith" (Mark 6:5 – 6). This is Jesus! The Son of God! With the power to heal! Anyone? It wasn't because Jesus lacked the ability to do the miracles. That was never the case. He wanted to perform miracles, but faith is a necessary ingredient. We have to want him to do them and believe that he can. There was a lack of faith in his hometown.

We've gotta move out in faith. Like the widow, we've gotta get up and go to the prophet. God can show up, but we've gotta believe we can change.

You might tell someone, "If God wants my life to change, he will make it happen." But the truth is that you keep doing the same thing you've always done. So guess what? You'll continue to get what you've always had. You're waiting for God to wave his magic wand over your life, your problems, and fix everything. But you do nothing. You don't really believe that your life can change. And you fail to "ask in faith" for God to step in to help you.

I get your doubts about all this. The widow initially had them ("I only have a little oil."). Moses had them ("Who am I? I can't speak!"). David had them, Paul had them, Ruth, Mary—everyone has doubts. I've had them more times than I can remember. But "we walk by faith, not by sight" (2 Cor. 5:7 KJV).

When Joshua was leading the Israelites through the Jordan River, God told them to first put their feet in the water. They did and the waters parted, just as God said they would. The ground was dry. Most of us wait for that river to part first, but God says, put your foot in the water. Then I will show up.

Keep the Faith

Perhaps no other passage of Scripture reveals this truth as comprehensively as the "Faith Hall of Fame" depicted in Hebrews. Here we find a definition of faith: "confidence in what we hope for and assurance about what we do not see" (Heb. 11:1), as well as numerous specific examples. In each one we can see a "but God" encounter, which I've summarized in italics after each person's experience.

By faith Abel brought God a better offering than Cain did. By faith he was commended as righteous, when God spoke well of his offerings. And by faith Abel still speaks, even though he is dead.

Abel suffered death at the hands of his brother, ***but God*** *honored Abel's offering and by faith his sacrifice lives on.*

By faith Enoch was taken from this life, so that he

did not experience death: "He could not be found, because God had taken him away." For before he was taken, he was commended as one who pleased God. And without faith it is impossible to please God, because anyone who comes to him must believe that he exists and that he rewards those who earnestly seek him.

*Enoch disappeared from this earth, **but God** brought him directly to heaven because of Enoch's faith.*

By faith Noah, when warned about things not yet seen, in holy fear built an ark to save his family. By his faith he condemned the world and became heir of the righteousness that is in keeping with faith.

*Noah could have perished in the flood, **but God** gave him divine instructions on how to survive, which Noah followed by faith.*

By faith Abraham, when called to go to a place he would later receive as his inheritance, obeyed and went, even though he did not know where he was going.

*Abraham didn't know where he was going, **but God** led him to the place where he would, by faith, become the father of the nation of Israel.*

And by faith even Sarah, who was past childbearing age, was enabled to bear children because she considered him faithful who had made the promise.

*Sarah was too old to have a child, **but God** allowed her to conceive a son because of her faith in God.*

By faith Isaac blessed Jacob and Esau in regard to their future.

*Isaac didn't know what lay in store for his twin sons, **but God** blessed them because of their father's faith.*

By faith Jacob, when he was dying, blessed each of Joseph's sons, and worshiped as he leaned on the top of his staff.

*Jacob made many mistakes during his life, **but God** redeemed him and changed his name to Israel.*

By faith Joseph, when his end was near, spoke about the exodus of the Israelites from Egypt and gave instructions concerning the burial of his bones.

*Joseph faced terrible ordeals, **but God** used them as stepping-stones to save the people of Israel during a famine.*

By faith Moses' parents hid him for three months after he was born, because they saw he was no ordinary child, and they were not afraid of the king's edict.

*Moses' parents knew their infant son was in danger, **but God** saved Moses' life because of his parents' faith.*

By faith Moses, when he had grown up, refused to be known as the son of Pharaoh's daughter. He chose to be mistreated along with the people of God rather than to enjoy the fleeting pleasures of sin. He regarded disgrace for the sake of Christ as of greater value than the treasures of Egypt, because he was looking ahead to his reward. By faith he left Egypt, not fearing the king's anger; he persevered because he saw him who is invisible. By faith he kept the Passover and the application of blood, so that the destroyer of the firstborn would not touch the first-born of Israel.

*Moses could have enjoyed his privileged status, **but God** called him to lead the Israelites out of Egypt by faith.*

By faith the people passed through the Red Sea as on dry land; but when the Egyptians tried to do so, they were drowned.

*The people of Israel suffered as slaves under Pharaoh, **but God** opened a route for their escape.*

By faith the walls of Jericho fell, after the army had marched around them for seven days.

*Joshua and the Israelites were outnumbered, **but God** instructed them on how to win in battle and possess the land.*

By faith the prostitute Rahab, because she welcomed the spies, was not killed with those who were disobedient.

*Rahab faced death and the destruction of her homeland, **but God** rescued her because of her faithful obedience.*

HEBREWS 11:4 – 34

And what more shall I say? I do not have time to tell about Gideon, Barak, Samson and Jephthah, about David and Samuel and the prophets, who through faith conquered kingdoms, administered justice, and gained what was promised; who shut the mouths of lions, quenched the fury of the flames, and escaped the edge of the sword; whose weakness was turned to strength; and who became powerful in battle and routed foreign armies.

These heroes of the faith are legendary for one reason and one reason only: they invited and embraced God's presence in their lives. They were no better than you or I. They struggled, failed, loved, lived, dreamed, laughed, failed some more, and loved God in the midst of it all. They encountered major "but God" experiences and by faith obeyed his instructions and were transformed.

Evidence of Hope

I know it's tempting to think, *Breaking free ... living free ... that's all great for you to talk about, but I'm doing the best I can. I live in the real world.* Maybe you've heard the "steps" you should take from Oprah or Dr. Phil. Or you've read self-help books and attended conferences. You've listened to your pastor's sermons. And still — you haven't changed. "I'm doing the best I know how."

I get that.

I grew up hearing that from a close family member. I lived in the shadow of that. I've said it myself quite a few times. I understand why you would believe that. But let me share a few final verses:

Be strong and take heart, all you who *hope* in the
LORD (Ps. 31:24, emphasis mine).

"But now, Lord, what do I look for? My *hope* is in
you" (Ps. 39:7, emphasis mine).

May the God of *hope* fill you with all joy and peace as
you trust in him, so that you may overflow with *hope*
by the power of the Holy Spirit (Rom. 15:13, emphasis mine).

There is surely a future *hope* for you, and your *hope*
will not be cut off (Prov. 23:18, emphasis mine).

But if we *hope* for what we do not see, we wait for it
with patience (Rom. 8:25 ESV, emphasis mine*).*

I'm sure you picked up on my not-so-subtle hint about
the thematic thread — *hope* — that is running through
each of these verses. Look at that last verse again and
notice the way hope relates to our Faith Hall of Fame.
Hebrews 11:1 says that faith is confidence in what we
HOPE for and assurance of things not seen. The key com-
ponent to having faith is having hope. You first have to
have hope that things can be different — that they can
change. This leads you into faith, which leads to taking
action and doing what you can do.

You have to have hope that things can change — that
they really, truly can change. Without hope, you won't
have faith. And without faith, you stop your "but God"
moment from ever happening. Without faith, we cannot
please God (Heb. 11:6). "But God" moments happen when
we have faith that somehow, in some way, God can show

up. He may not show up the way we want or exactly when we want, but God never abandons us. No matter what we're experiencing or how low we've fallen, God can show up and begin a "but God" transformation in our lives.

In your pocket, you might have two dollars. But God can show up and multiply those dollars into millions.

You might have an addiction to shopping or alcohol or drugs. But God can show up and free you.

Your job may be at a dead end, but God can show up and revive your career.

You may be in an abusive dating relationship and think you have to stay because no one else will ever love you. But God can bring a godly person into your life who will treat you with the dignity and love you deserve.

You have to have hope that God can change your life because he can!

He restores broken relationships.

He mends the broken heart.

He heals sick bodies.

He provides water from a rock.

He opens up the Red Sea.

God does the impossible.

You've got to believe that! It's possible! Stop believing *But God, I can't*, and start knowing *But God I can*.

But God changes *everything*, and he can change your life!

God can turn your situation around. I'm living proof! I should be in jail ... *but God*. I should be an unfaithful husband ... *but God*. I should be divorced ... *but God*. I should be broke ... *but God*. I should be a statistic ... *but God*. I should be bitter and angry ... *but God*!

Are you ready for God to change your life? He is waiting to see your faith and to meet you there. Put one foot down, and then put the other foot down in front of it. When you do, *God will meet you.*

"But God" is not just a catchphrase; it's not just a title you might remember. "But God" really is true! It's the essence of how God intervenes and rescues us, redeems and radically transforms us. So take another step. There is hope. There is freedom. There is a bright future when you just trust him.

"But God" changes everything!

"**But God**" Verses in the Holy Bible, KJV

1. **GENESIS 20:3:** *But God* came to Abimelech in a dream by night, and said to him, Behold, thou art but a dead man, for the woman which thou hast taken; for she is a man's wife.[7]

2. **GENESIS 31:7:** And your father hath deceived me, and changed my wages ten times; *but God* suffered him not to hurt me.

3. **GENESIS 45:8:** So now it was not you that sent me hither, *but God*: and he hath made me a father to Pharaoh, and lord of all his house, and a ruler throughout all the land of Egypt.

4. **GENESIS 48:21:** And Israel said unto Joseph, Behold, I die: *but God* shall be with you, and bring you again unto the land of your fathers.

5. **GENESIS 50:20:** But as for you, ye thought evil against

me: *but God* meant it unto good, to bring to pass, as it is this day, to save much people alive.

6. **EXODUS 13:18:** *But God* led the people about, through the way of the wilderness of the Red sea: and the children of Israel went up harnessed out of the land of Egypt.

7. **EXODUS 21:13:** And if a man lie not in wait, *but God* deliver him into his hand; then I will appoint thee a place whither he shall flee.

8. **JUDGES 15:19:** *But God* clave an hollow place that was in the jaw, and there came water thereout; and when he had drunk, his spirit came again, and he revived: wherefore he called the name thereof Enhakkore, which is in Lehi unto this day.

9. **1 SAMUEL 23:14:** And David abode in the wilderness in strong holds, and remained in a mountain in the wilderness of Ziph. And Saul sought him every day, *but God* delivered him not into his hand.

10. **1 CHRONICLES 28:3:** *But God* said unto me, Thou shalt not build an house for my name, because thou hast been a man of war, and hast shed blood.

11. **PSALM 49:15:** *But God* will redeem my soul from the power of the grave: for he shall receive me. Selah.

12. **PSALM 64:7:** *But God* shall shoot at them with an arrow; suddenly shall they be wounded.

13. **PSALM 68:21:** *But God* shall wound the head of his enemies, and the hairy scalp of such an one as goeth on still in his trespasses.

14. **PSALM 73:26:** My flesh and my heart faileth: *but God* is the strength of my heart, and my portion for ever.

15. **PSALM 75:7:** *But God* is the judge: he putteth down one, and setteth up another.

16. **PROVERBS 21:12:** The righteous man wisely considereth the house of the wicked: *but God* overthroweth the wicked for their wickedness.

17. **ISAIAH 17:13:** The nations shall rush like the rushing of many waters: *but God* shall rebuke them, and they shall flee far off, and shall be chased as the chaff of the mountains before the wind, and like a rolling thing before the whirlwind.

18. **JONAH 4:7:** *But God* prepared a worm when the morning rose the next day, and it smote the gourd that it withered.

19. **MARK 2:7:** Why doth this man thus speak blasphemies? who can forgive sins *but God* only?

20. **LUKE 5:21:** And the scribes and the Pharisees began to reason, saying, Who is this which speaketh blasphemies? Who can forgive sins, *but God* alone?

21. **LUKE 12:20:** *But God* said unto him, Thou fool, this night thy soul shall be required of thee: then whose shall those things be, which thou hast provided?

22. **LUKE 16:15:** And he said unto them, Ye are they which justify yourselves before men; *but God* knoweth your hearts: for that which is highly esteemed among men is abomination in the sight of God.

23. **ACTS 7:9:** And the patriarchs, moved with envy, sold Joseph into Egypt: *but God* was with him.

24. **ACTS 10:28:** And he said unto them, Ye know how that it is an unlawful thing for a man that is a Jew to keep company, or come unto one of another nation; *but God* hath shewed me that I should not call any man common or unclean.

25. **ACTS 13:30:** *But God* raised him from the dead.

26. **ROMANS 5:8:** *But God* commendeth his love toward us, in that, while we were yet sinners, Christ died for us.

27. **ROMANS 6:17:** *But God* be thanked, that ye were the servants of sin, but ye have obeyed from the heart that form of doctrine which was delivered you.

28. **1 CORINTHIANS 1:27:** *But God* hath chosen the foolish things of the world to confound the wise; and God hath chosen the weak things of the world to confound the things which are mighty.

29. **1 CORINTHIANS 2:10:** *But God* hath revealed them unto us by his Spirit: for the Spirit searcheth all things, yea, the deep things of God.

30. **1 CORINTHIANS 3:6:** I have planted, Apollos watered; *but God* gave the increase.

31. **1 CORINTHIANS 3:7:** So then neither is he that planteth any thing, neither he that watereth; *but God* that giveth the increase.

32. **1 CORINTHIANS 6:13:** Meats for the belly, and the belly for meats: *but God* shall destroy both it and

them. Now the body is not for fornication, but for the Lord; and the Lord for the body.

33. **1 CORINTHIANS 7:15:** But if the unbelieving depart, let him depart. A brother or a sister is not under bondage in such cases: *but God* hath called us to peace.

34. **1 CORINTHIANS 10:13:** There hath no temptation taken you but such as is common to man: *but God* is faithful, who will not suffer you to be tempted above that ye are able; but will with the temptation also make a way to escape, that ye may be able to bear it.

35. **1 CORINTHIANS 12:24:** For our comely parts have no need: *but God* hath tempered the body together, having given more abundant honour to that part which lacked.

36. **1 CORINTHIANS 15:38:** *But God* giveth it a body as it hath pleased him, and to every seed his own body.

37. **GALATIANS 3:18:** For if the inheritance be of the law, it is no more of promise: *but God* gave it to Abraham by promise.

38. **GALATIANS 3:20:** Now a mediator is not a mediator of one, *but God* is one.

39. **GALATIANS 6:14:** *But God* forbid that I should glory, save in the cross of our Lord Jesus Christ, by whom the world is crucified unto me, and I unto the world.

40. **EPHESIANS 2:4:** *But God*, who is rich in mercy, for his great love wherewith he loved us.

41. **PHILIPPIANS 2:27:** For indeed he was sick nigh unto death: *but God* had mercy on him; and not on him

only, but on me also, lest I should have sorrow upon sorrow.

42. **1 THESSALONIANS 2:4:** But as we were allowed of God to be put in trust with the gospel, even so we speak; not as pleasing men, *but God*, which trieth our hearts.

43. **1 THESSALONIANS 4:8:** He therefore that despiseth, despiseth not man, *but God*, who hath also given unto us his holy Spirit.

Acknowledgments

To everyone who encouraged me and offered assistance on this project, I'm so thankful for you and your support. I'm especially indebted to the following people:

Shane Hood: Thank you for being an incredible assistant and helping me with this book and with so many other projects.

Craig Groeschel: For believing in me, sharing my story, and consistently encouraging me to write a book, I thank you. I wouldn't have ever written this book without your support.

Tom Winters: You gave me the confidence to write this book. I'm grateful for your belief and wisdom.

Alicia Kelly: Thank you for your incredible work and help on the front end of this book. You and Terry are amazing people and amazing friends to Tiffany and me.

Dudley Delffs: You are a rock star. Thank you for your editorial expertise on this project.

Sandra Vander Zicht and the entire Zondervan team: You believed in this book FROM the moment I met you all at Catalyst. Thank you for supporting *But God.*

People's Church family: We've experienced so many "but God" moments together. I'm honored to be your pastor. We're FAMILY! The best is yet to come!

People's Church staff: I can't believe I get to do life and ministry with some of the finest people on the planet. Thank you for your dedication to God and his church.

Cale, Cade, Caris, Case: I love you more than you'll ever know. Being a dad to you four kids is truly one of the joys of my life. I'll always be your Sushi Bushi.

Tiffany Cooper: I can't put into words how much you mean to me. You are a Proverbs 31 woman. I adore you, cherish you, and love you deeply!

Notes

1. Joyce Meyer, "Three Steps to Emotional Healing That Lasts," http://www.joycemeyer.org/articles/ea.aspx?article=three_steps_to_emotional_healing_that_lasts.

2. C. S. Lewis, *The Weight of Glory* (San Francisco: HarperOne, 2009), 42.

3. Martin Luther, quoted at *ThinkExist.com*, http://thinkexist.com/quotation/all_who_call_on_god_in_true_faith-earnestly_from/164467.html.

4. "Tempt," definition from *Dictionary.com*, http://dictionary.reference.com/browse/tempted.

5. Oswald Chambers, "September 17," *My Utmost for His Highest* (Grand Rapids: Discovery House, 1992), 290.

6. Mark Twain, quoted at *The Quotations Page*, http://www.quotationspage.com/quote/41949.html.

7. Emphasis added throughout this section.

Herbert Cooper shares his amazing testimony in *But God*. We all face obstacles in life, and this book will encourage you as Herbert unpacks how the power of God can change any situation. No matter the challenge, *But God* changes everything!

MARK BATTERSON, bestselling author of *The Circle Maker* and lead pastor of National Community Church

Herbert Cooper is a fresh and powerful voice for faith today and it shows in this incredible book. *But God* is a must-read that delivers brilliant insight, brimming with hope. This book is meant to be savored personally and shared with others.

JUD WILHITE, author *Pursued*, senior pastor Central Christian Church

The one word that describes the book *But God* is hope. As Herbert Cooper shares his own story of pain you will discover that the redeeming power of God can change any situation. *But God* will encourage you, inspire you, and give you biblical perspective on life's toughest challenges.

STEVEN FURTICK, lead pastor, Elevation Church, and *New York Times* bestselling author of *Crash the Chatterbox*, *Greater*, and *Sun Stand Still*

But God could possibly be two of the most powerful words in the Bible. Herbert unpacks how we use those words as a bridge to get from where we are to where God wants to take us. This book will change your life.

STOVALL WEEMS, lead pastor, Celebration Church

But God ...Changes Everything reveals the essence of our hope in the power of God's love to transform our lives. With stories from his own life that will crack you up, along with insightful exploration of the Bible's least likely heroes, Herbert Cooper inspires you to invite God's healing presence into your hardest struggles and darkest secrets. *But God* is a handbook of hope for anyone longing to trust God in every area of their lives.

CHRIS HODGES, senior pastor, Church of the Highlands, author of *Fresh Air* and *Four Cups*

In *But God*, Herbert Cooper unflinchingly tells his own story of pain and redemption. The gospel is the good news that our struggles are never the end of the story. *But God* is the reminder we need that there is always hope.

GREG SURRATT, founding pastor, Seacoast Church

We are used to having all the resources we need to solve our problems on our own. But those who truly know God have learned to rejoice when everything looks bleak, when problems look impossible ... because these moments are the beginning of a "but God" story. Pastor Herbert lays out the uncomfortable, glorious reality that our First World problems mask a fundamental need for a Savior who will be there in the moments when all hope is lost. This book will confidently lead you into the exhilarating safety of a God who invades, intervenes, and provides on behalf of his children.

SCOTT WILLIAMS, church growth/leadership consultant and strategist at NxtLevel Solutions, author of *Church Diversity* and *Go Big*, @ScottWilliams

Herbert Cooper is an amazing testimony of God's redemption. His life is an example of someone who faced many challenges and has overcome them all. This book will transform how you think about your situation and will equip you with powerful tools and hope that God can turn any obstacle into a victory in your life.

PASTOR JOE CHAMPION, Celebration Church, Austin, TX

There is no obstacle or challenge we face in life that a "but God" moment can't overcome. In this book, Herbert Cooper shares how "but God" moments transformed his life of brokenness into a life of wholeness. Throughout the pages of this book, you will discover that God can turn any hopeless situation into hope-filled victory. This book is a must-read. *But God* truly changes everything!

ROBERT MADU, international evangelist